A Systematic Approach to Exa Diagnosis & Manual Therapy of the Wrist Part I

IAOM-US Course Outline:

Day 1

8:00-8:30 am	Introductions: instructors, participants, IAOM-US	
8:30-9:55 am	Anatomy and kinesiology-I	Lecture
9:55-10:10 am	**BREAK**	
10:10-11:00 am	Anatomy and kinesiology-II	Lecture
11:00-12:15 pm	Anatomy and kinesiology-III Lecture	
12:15-1:15 pm	**LUNCH**	
1:15-2:30 pm	Bony surface anatomy	Lab
2:30-4:30 pm	Basic clinical exam	Lecture/Lab
4:30-4:45 pm	**BREAK**	
4:45-5:30 pm	complete BCE of wrist	Lab
5:30-6:30 pm	Testing and treatment of the radiocarpal joint (RCJ) and midcarpal joints (MCJ)	Lab

Day 2

8:00-9:45 am	complete RCJ and MCJ mobilization techniques	Lab
9:45-9:55 am	**BREAK**	
9:55-11:00 am	Forearm rotation limitations: testing and treatment (DRUJ and PRUJ)	Lab
11:00-11:35 am	Surface anatomy: soft tissue structures of the wrist	Lab
11:35-12:05 pm	**LUNCH**	
12:05-2:00 pm	Soft tissues disorders: step-by-step from BCE, (de Quervain's, intersection syndrome, Wartenberg's, ECU tenosynovitis, ECRB/ECRL, FCU, FCR)-findings of BCE, interpretation, treatment suggestions; screen for Thoracic Outlet Syndrome	Lecture
2:00-2:40 pm	Graded Motor Imagery	Lecture
2:40-2:50 pm	Case studies	
2:50-3:00 pm	**QUESTIONS & CLOSING REMARKS**	

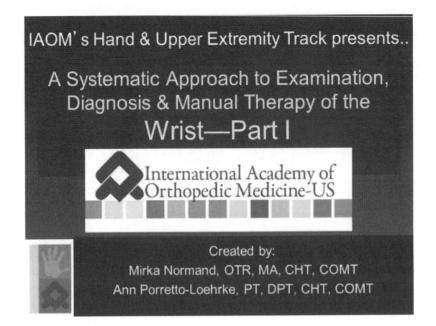

Picture 1: Slide1

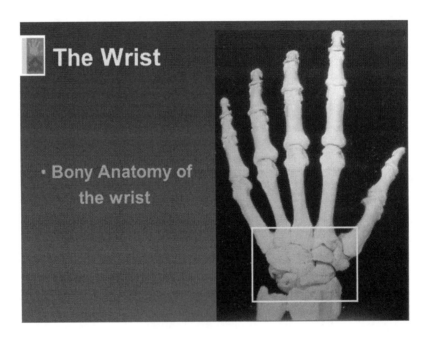

Picture 2: Slide2

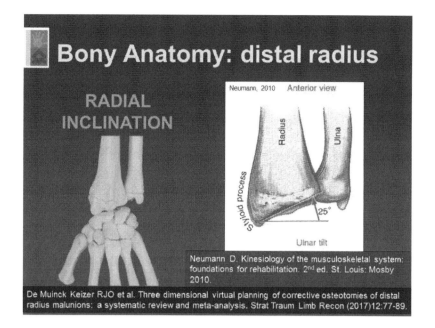

Picture 3: Slide3

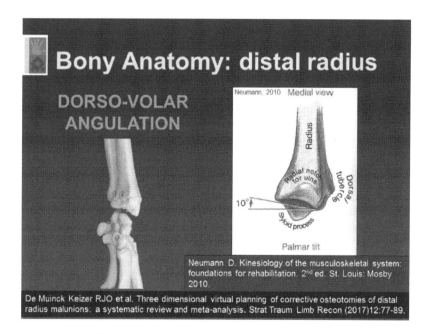

Picture 4: Slide4

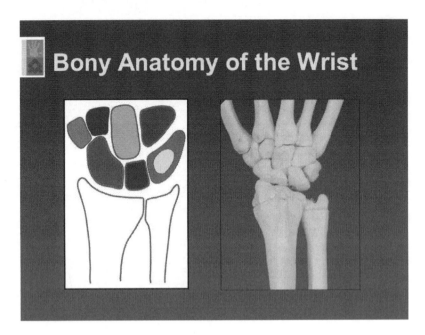

Picture 5: Slide5

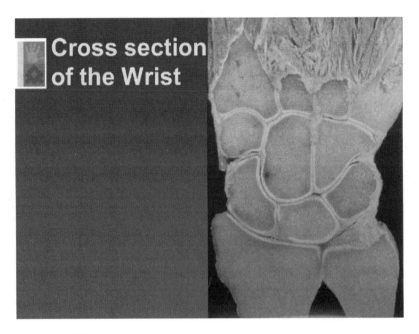

Picture 6: Slide6

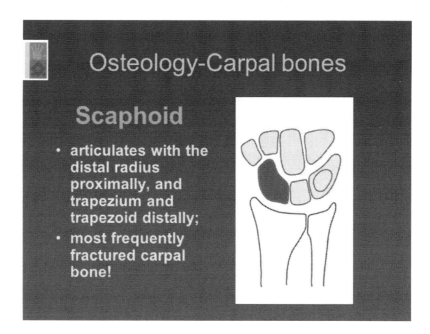

Picture 7: Slide7

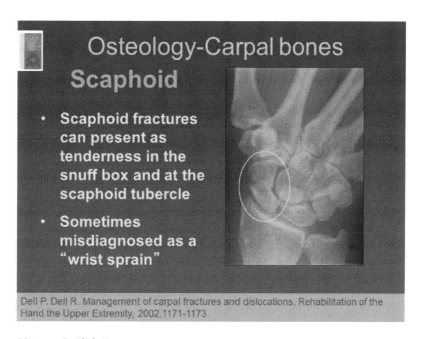

Picture 8: Slide8

Osteology-Carpal bones
Scaphoid

- Waist fractures are the most common

- The proximal pole relies entirely on intramedullary blood flow

- This unusual nature of retrograde blood supply renders the proximal pole susceptible to vascular necrosis following a waist fracture

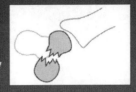

Gupta V et al. Management of scaphoid fractures: how we do it?. J clin orth and trauma (2013)4:3-10.

Picture 9: Slide9

Osteology-Carpal bones
Scaphoid

Times to union increasing for more proximal frx;

- distal third frx: 6-8 wks;

- middle third frx: 8-12 wks;

- proximal third frx: 12-23 wks;

However, may not be diagnosed until 2-3 weeks post fracture

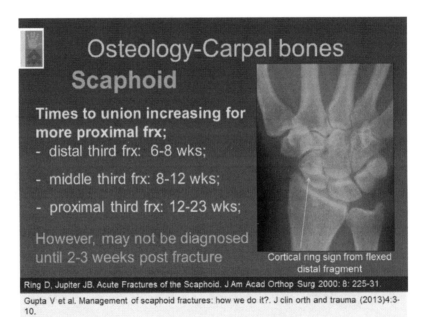

Cortical ring sign from flexed distal fragment

Ring D, Jupiter JB. Acute Fractures of the Scaphoid. J Am Acad Orthop Surg 2000: 8: 225-31.

Gupta V et al. Management of scaphoid fractures: how we do it?. J clin orth and trauma (2013)4:3-10.

Picture 10: Slide10

Osteology-Carpal bones
Scaphoid

Treatment is based on location and degree of displacement.

Surgical percutaneous treatment of non-displaced fractures can also be performed to decrease immobilization time and to allow early range of motion.

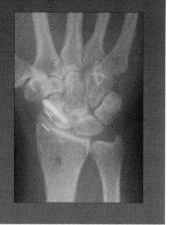

Gupta V et al. Management of scaphoid fractures: how we do it?. J clin orth and trauma (2013)4:3-10.

Picture 11: Slide11

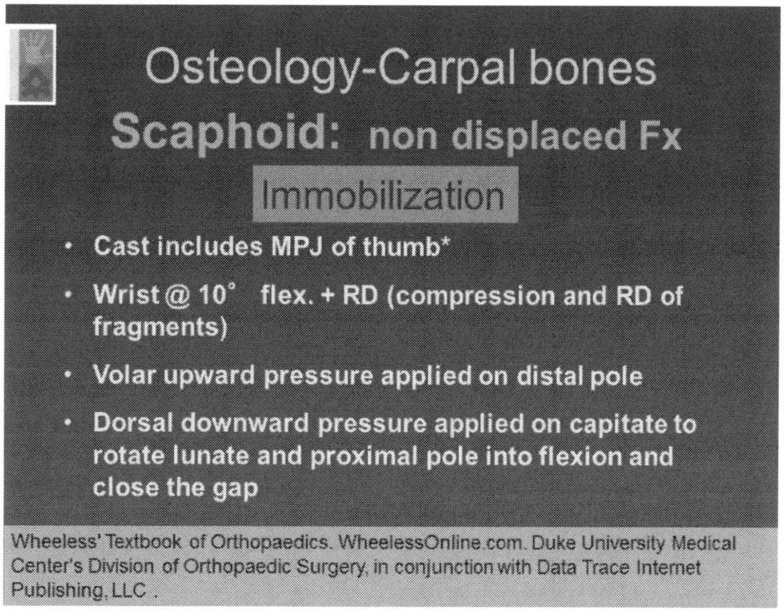

Osteology-Carpal bones
Scaphoid: non displaced Fx
Immobilization

- Cast includes MPJ of thumb*

- Wrist @ 10° flex. + RD (compression and RD of fragments)

- Volar upward pressure applied on distal pole

- Dorsal downward pressure applied on capitate to rotate lunate and proximal pole into flexion and close the gap

Wheeless' Textbook of Orthopaedics. WheelessOnline.com. Duke University Medical Center's Division of Orthopaedic Surgery, in conjunction with Data Trace Internet Publishing, LLC .

Picture 12: Slide12

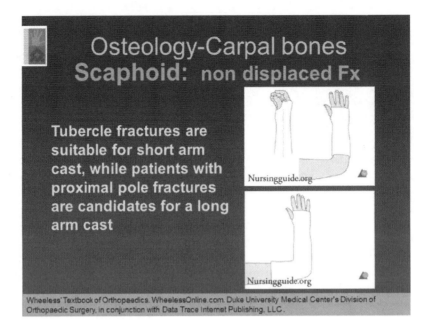

Picture 13: Slide13

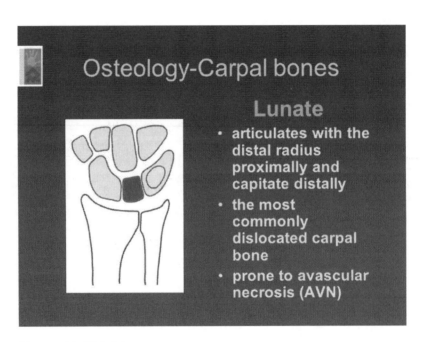

Picture 14: Slide14

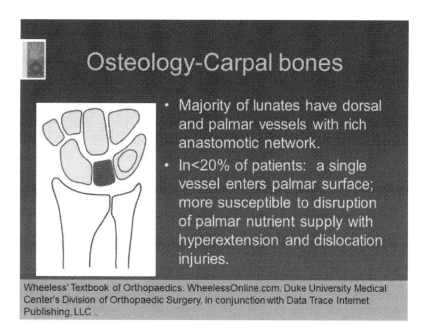

Osteology-Carpal bones

- Majority of lunates have dorsal and palmar vessels with rich anastomotic network.
- In<20% of patients: a single vessel enters palmar surface; more susceptible to disruption of palmar nutrient supply with hyperextension and dislocation injuries.

Wheeless' Textbook of Orthopaedics. WheelessOnline.com. Duke University Medical Center's Division of Orthopaedic Surgery, in conjunction with Data Trace Internet Publishing, LLC .

Picture 15: Slide15

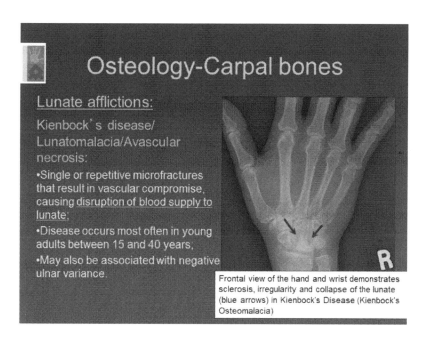

Osteology-Carpal bones

Lunate afflictions:

Kienbock's disease/ Lunatomalacia/Avascular necrosis:

- Single or repetitive microfractures that result in vascular compromise, causing disruption of blood supply to lunate;
- Disease occurs most often in young adults between 15 and 40 years;
- May also be associated with negative ulnar variance.

Frontal view of the hand and wrist demonstrates sclerosis, irregularity and collapse of the lunate (blue arrows) in Kienbock's Disease (Kienbock's Osteomalacia)

Picture 16: Slide16

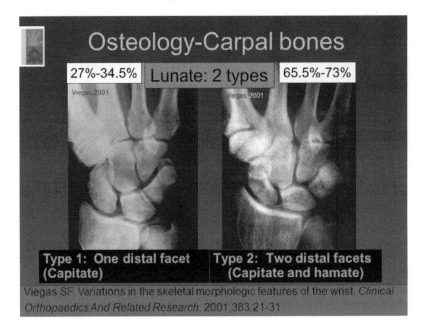

Picture 17: Slide17

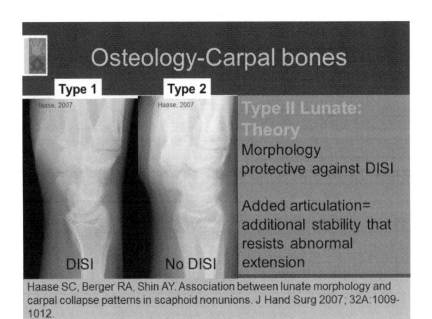

Picture 18: Slide18

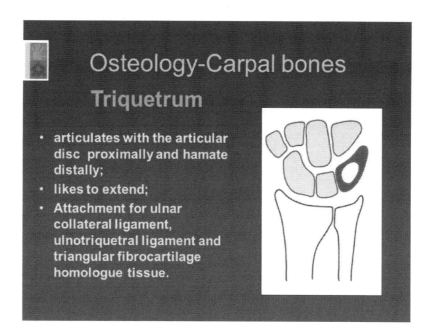

Picture 19: Slide19

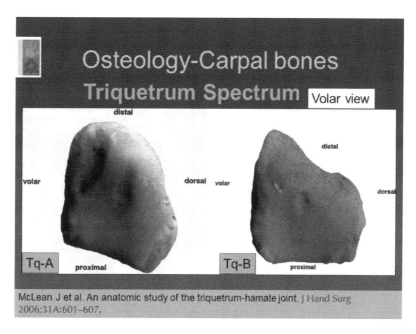

Picture 20: Slide20

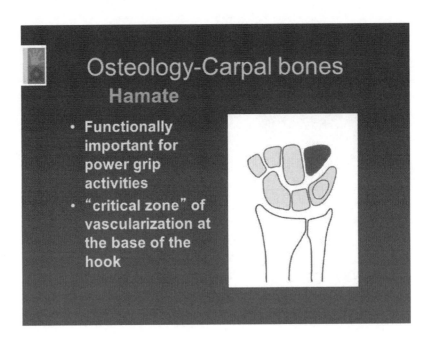

Picture 21: Slide21

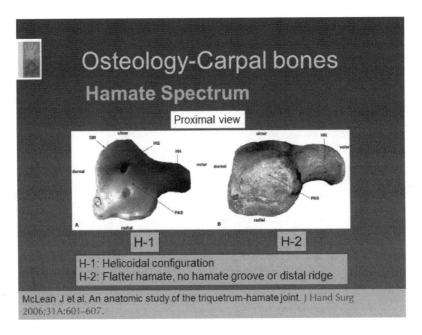

Picture 22: Slide22

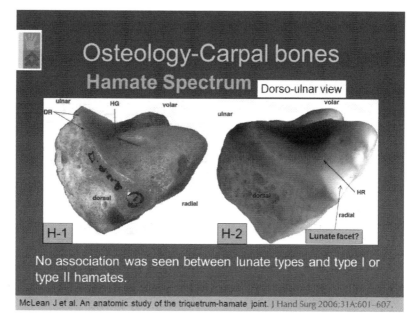

Picture 23: Slide23

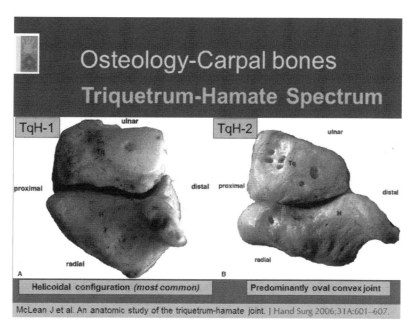

Picture 24: Slide24

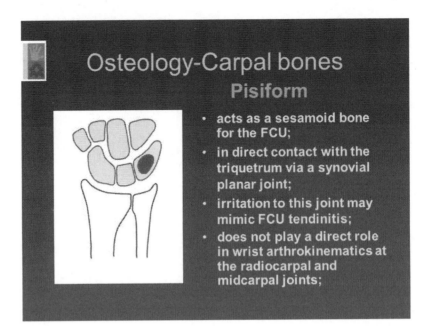

Picture 25: Slide25

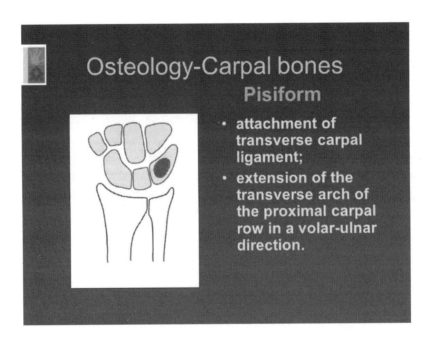

Picture 26: Slide26

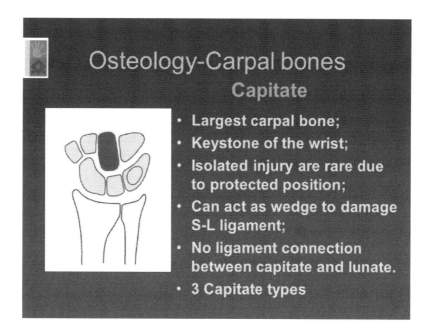

Picture 27: Slide27

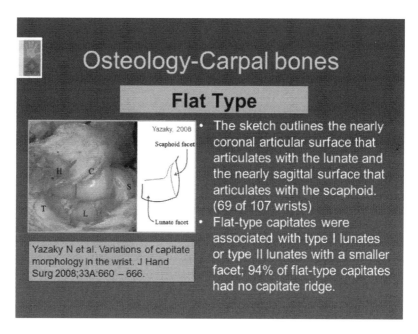

Picture 28: Slide28

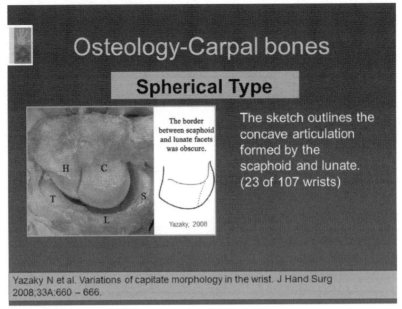

Picture 29: Slide29

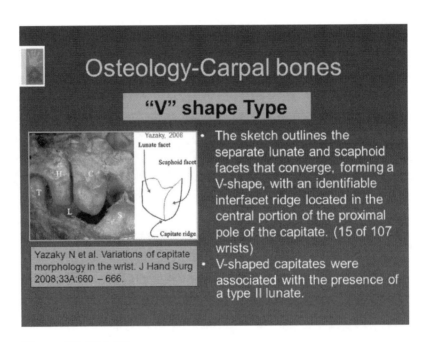

Picture 30: Slide30

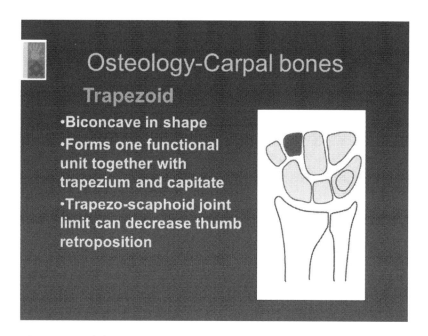

Picture 31: Slide31

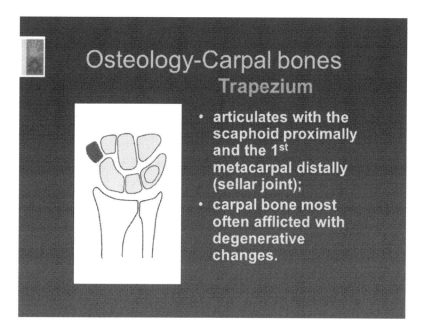

Picture 32: Slide32

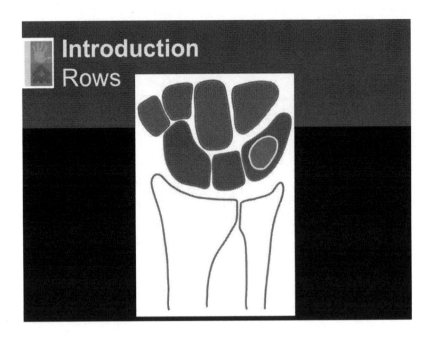

Picture 33: Slide33

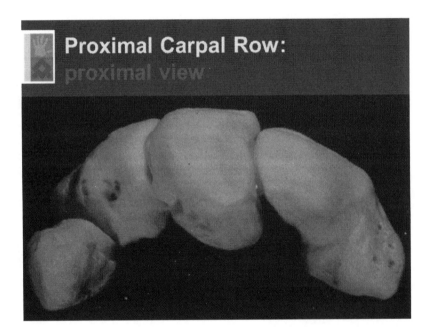

Picture 34: Slide34

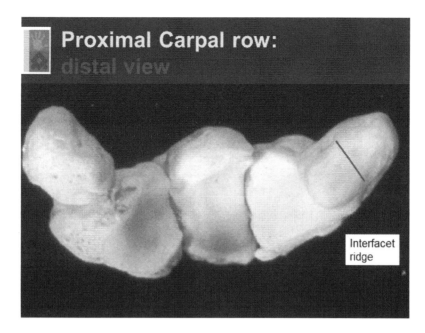

Picture 35: Slide35

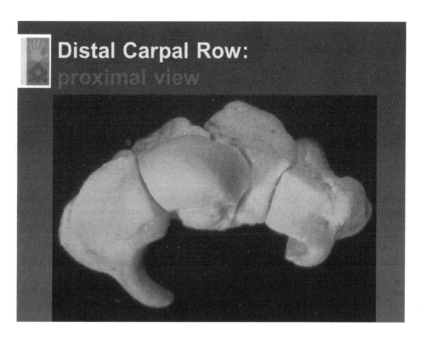

Picture 36: Slide36

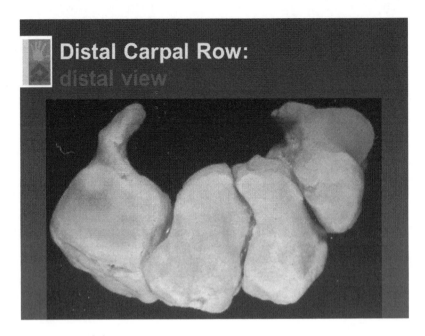

Picture 37: Slide37

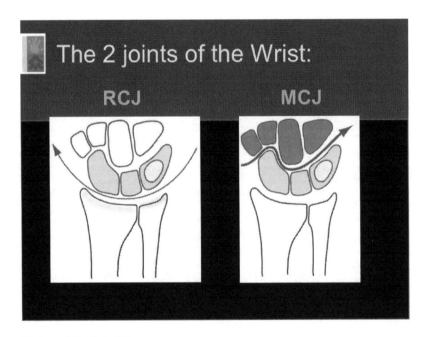

Picture 38: Slide38

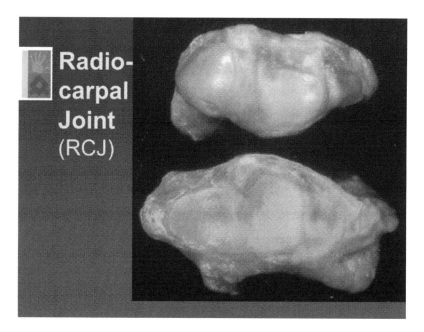

Picture 39: Slide39

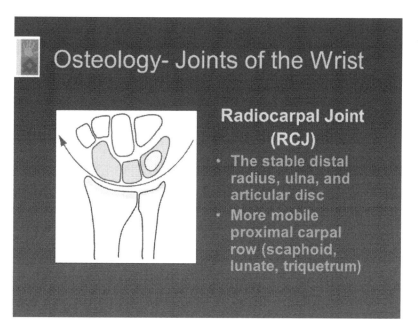

Picture 40: Slide40

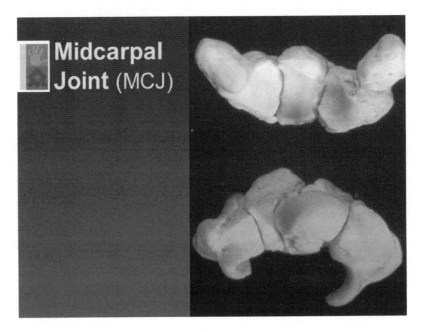

Picture 41: Slide41

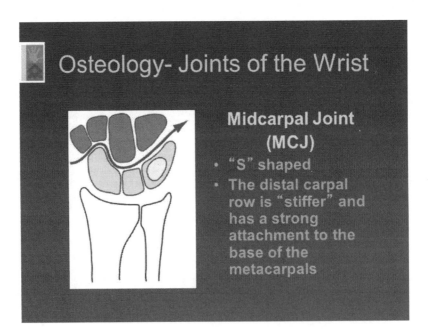

Picture 42: Slide42

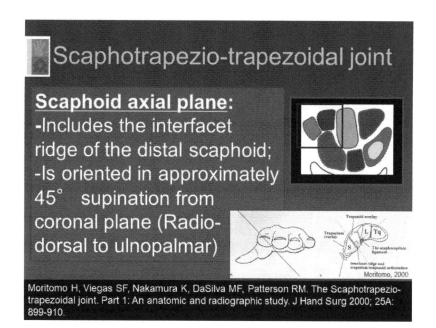

Picture 43: Slide43

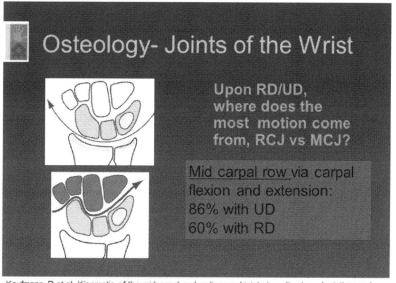

Picture 44: Slide44

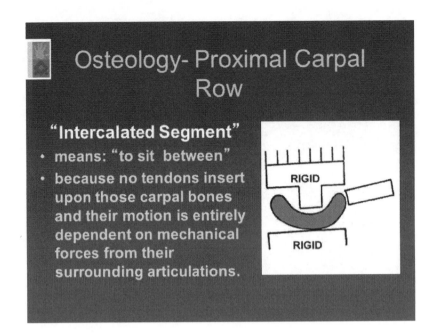

Picture 45: Slide45

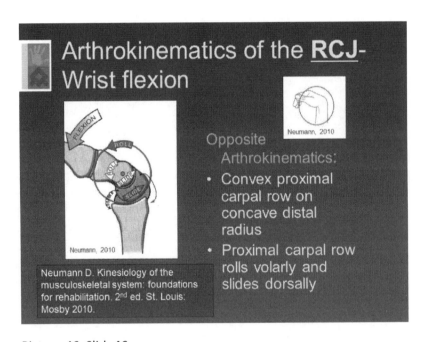

Picture 46: Slide46

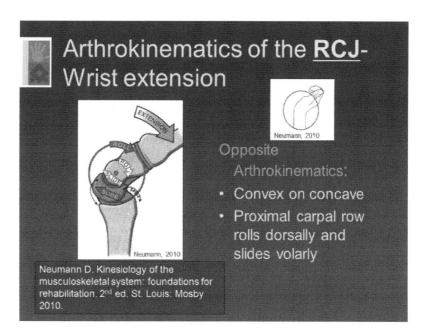

Picture 47: Slide47

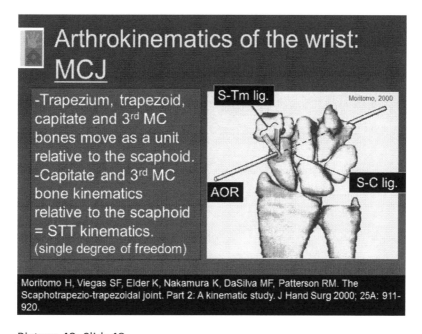

Picture 48: Slide48

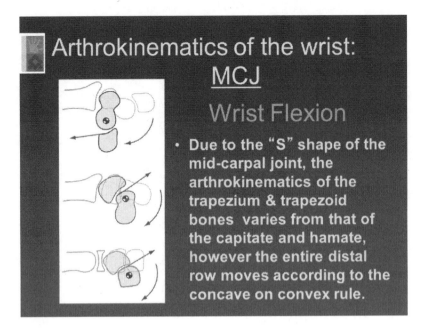

Arthrokinematics of the wrist: MCJ

Wrist Flexion

- Due to the "S" shape of the mid-carpal joint, the arthrokinematics of the trapezium & trapezoid bones varies from that of the capitate and hamate, however the entire distal row moves according to the concave on convex rule.

Picture 49: Slide49

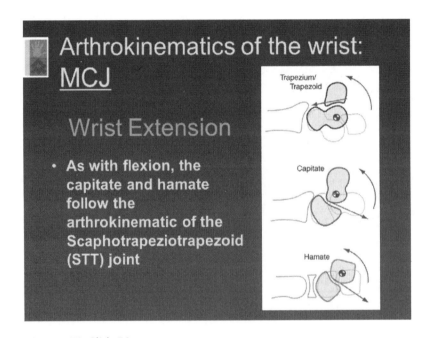

Arthrokinematics of the wrist: MCJ

Wrist Extension

- As with flexion, the capitate and hamate follow the arthrokinematic of the Scaphotrapeziotrapezoid (STT) joint

Picture 50: Slide50

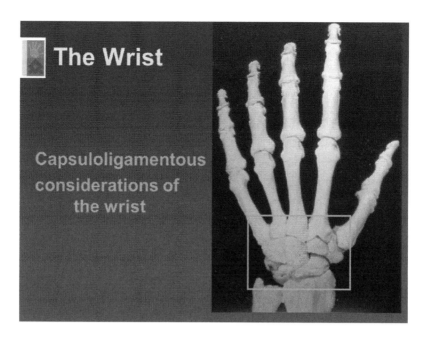

Picture 51: Slide1

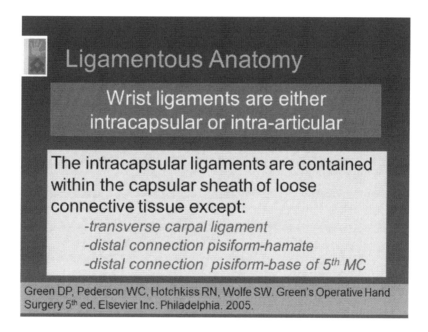

Picture 52: Slide2

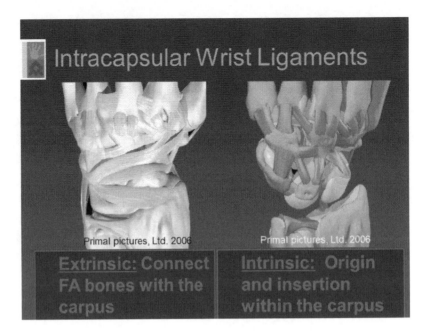

Picture 53: Slide3

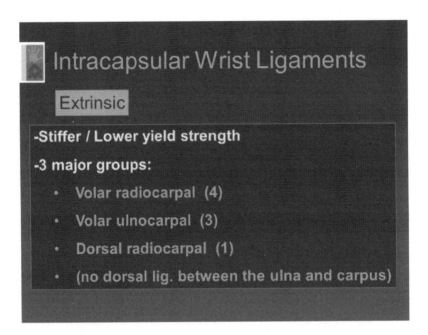

Picture 54: Slide4

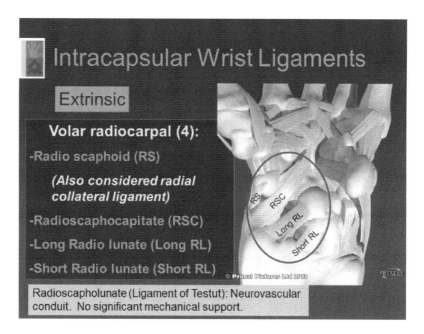

Picture 55: Slide5

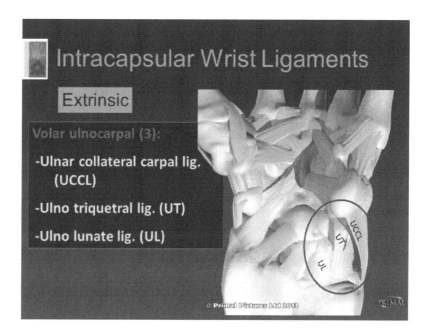

Picture 56: Slide6

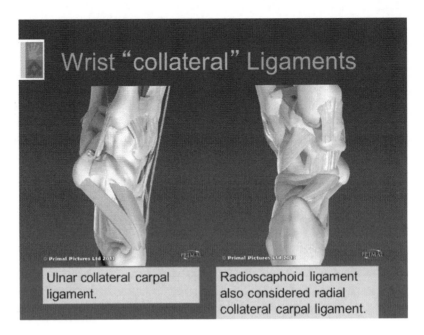

Picture 57: Slide7

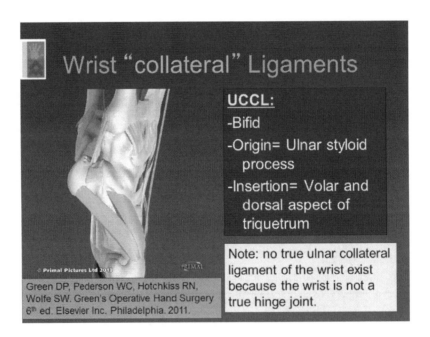

Picture 58: Slide8

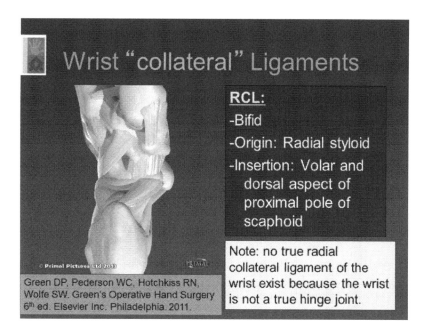

Picture 59: Slide9

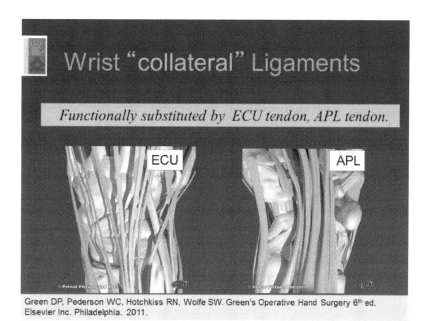

Picture 60: Slide10

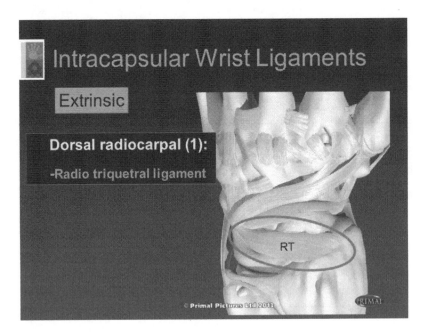

Picture 61: Slide11

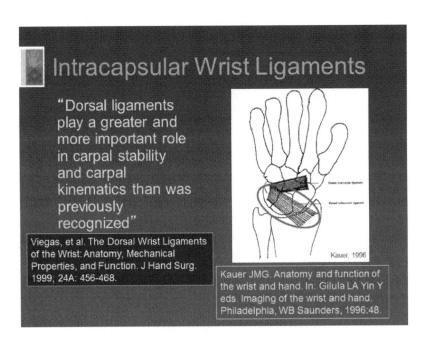

Picture 62: Slide12

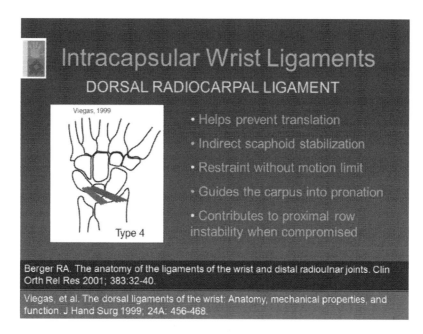

Picture 63: Slide13

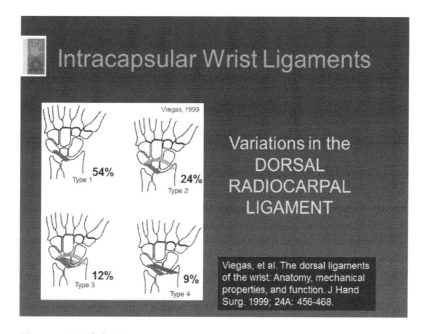

Picture 64: Slide14

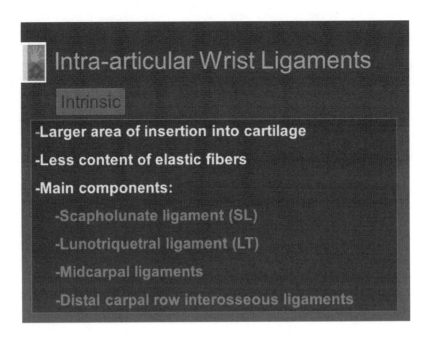

Picture 65: Slide15

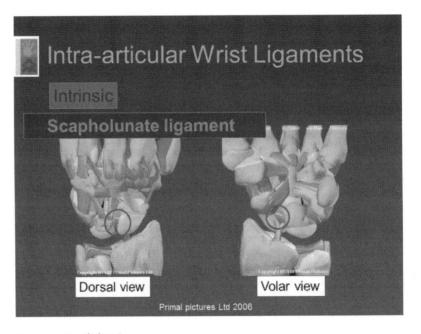

Picture 66: Slide16

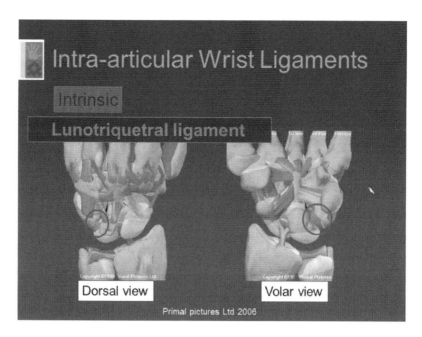

Picture 67: Slide17

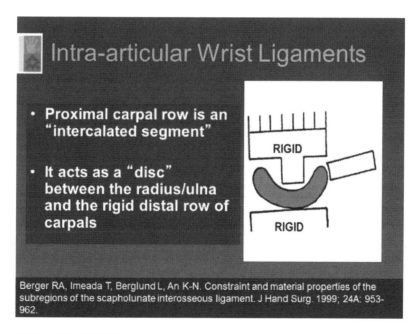

Picture 68: Slide18

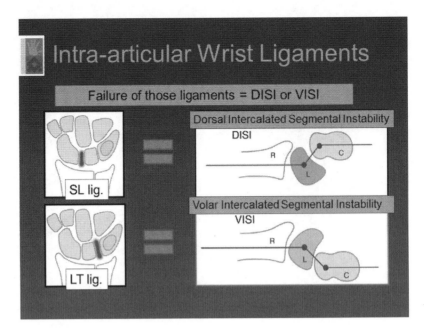

Picture 69: Slide19

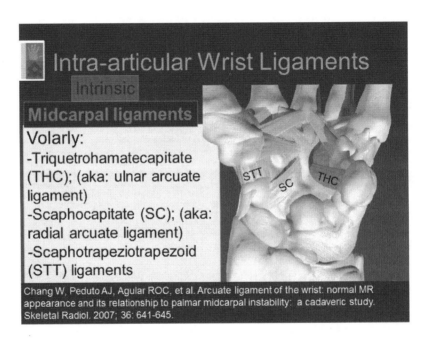

Picture 70: Slide20

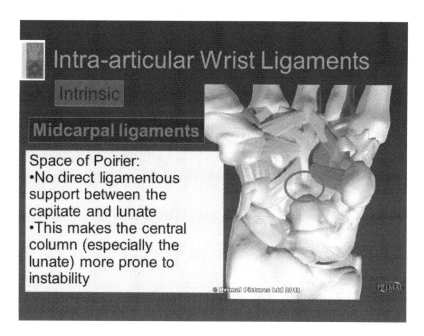

Picture 71: Slide21

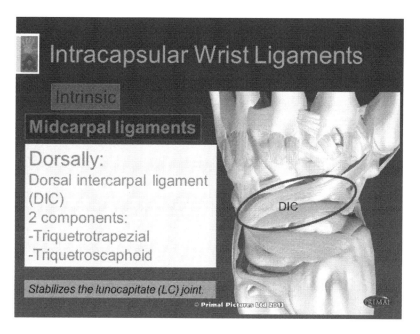

Picture 72: Slide22

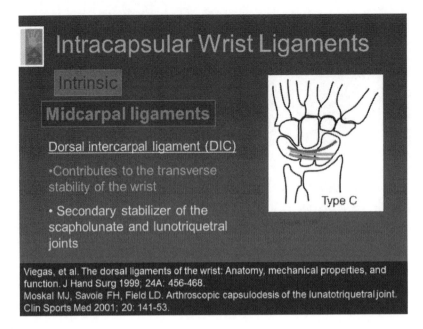

Picture 73: Slide23

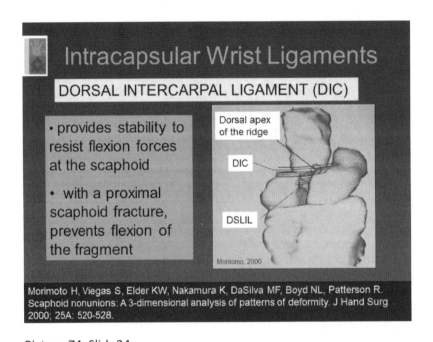

Picture 74: Slide24

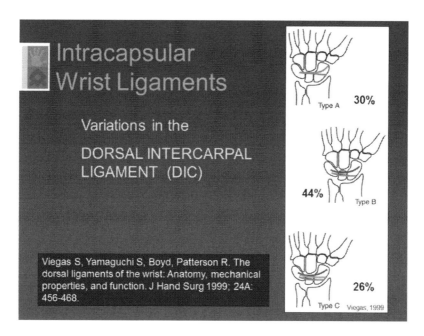

Picture 75: Slide25

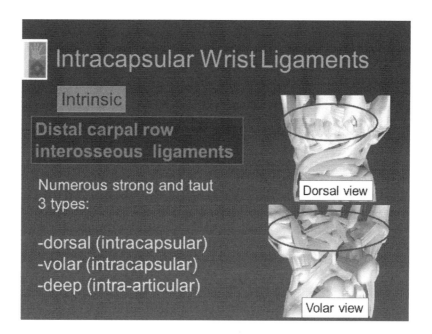

Picture 76: Slide26

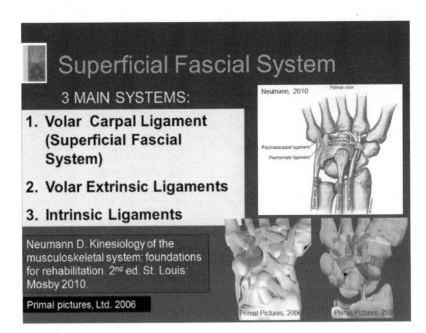

Picture 77: Slide27

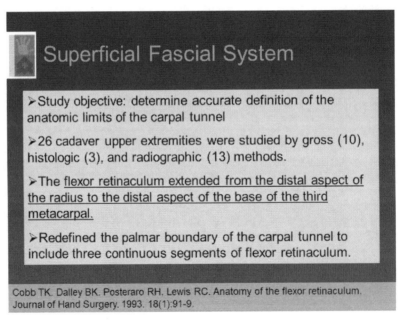

Picture 78: Slide28

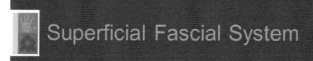

Superficial Fascial System

Three continuous segments of flexor retinaculum (volarly):
-Thin proximal segment composed of thickened deep investing fascia of the forearm;
-Transverse carpal ligament;
-Distal portion composed of an aponeurosis between the thenar and hypothenar muscles.

Cobb TK. Dalley BK. Posteraro RH. Lewis RC. Anatomy of the flexor retinaculum. Journal of Hand Surgery. 1993. 18(1):91-9.

Picture 79: Slide29

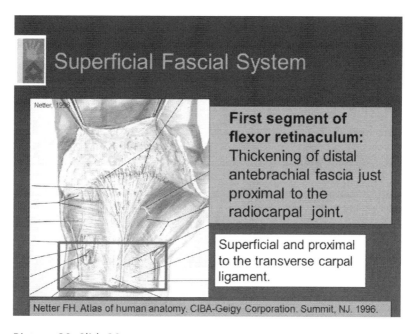

Superficial Fascial System

First segment of flexor retinaculum:
Thickening of distal antebrachial fascia just proximal to the radiocarpal joint.

Superficial and proximal to the transverse carpal ligament.

Netter FH. Atlas of human anatomy. CIBA-Geigy Corporation. Summit, NJ. 1996.

Picture 80: Slide30

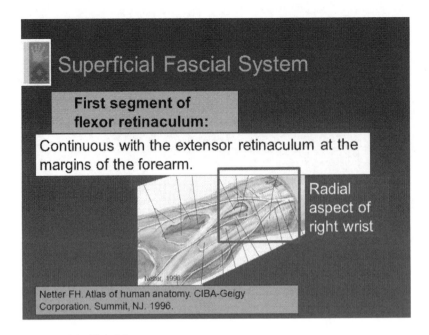

Picture 81: Slide31

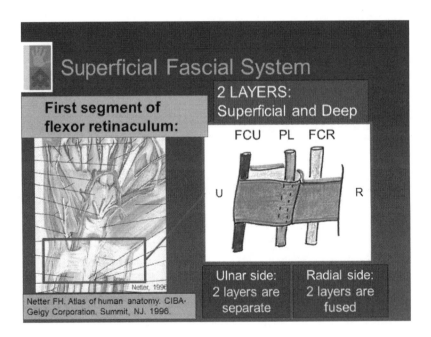

Picture 82: Slide32

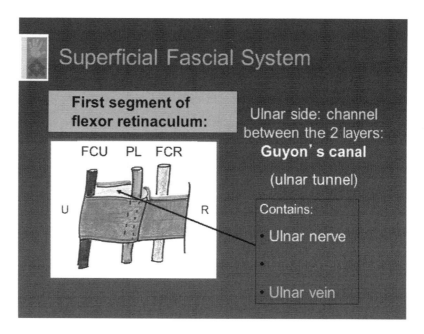

Picture 83: Slide33

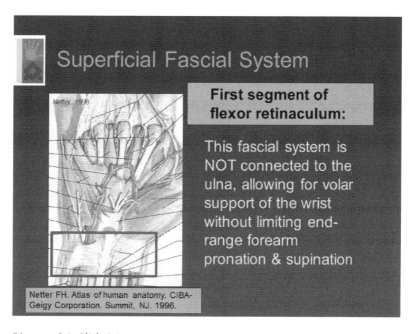

Picture 84: Slide34

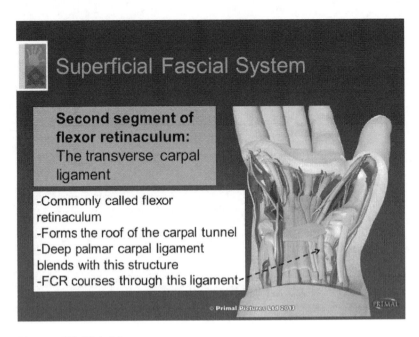

Picture 85: Slide35

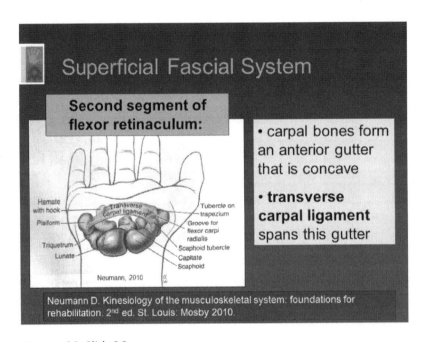

Picture 86: Slide36

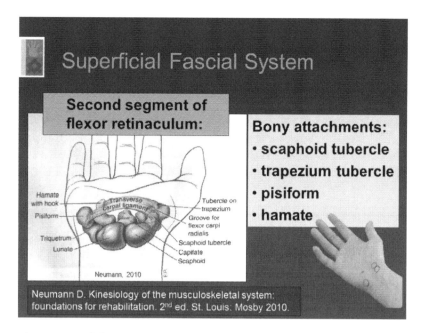

Picture 87: Slide37

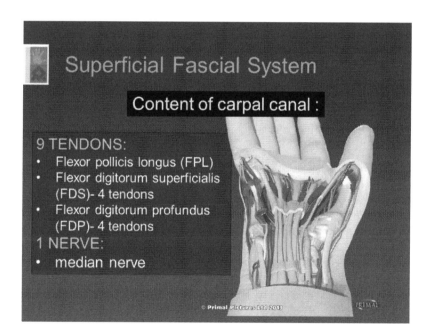

Picture 88: Slide38

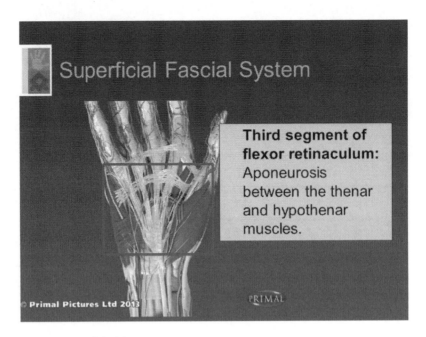

Picture 89: Slide39

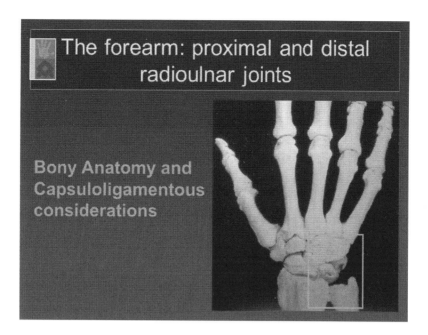

Picture 90: Slide1

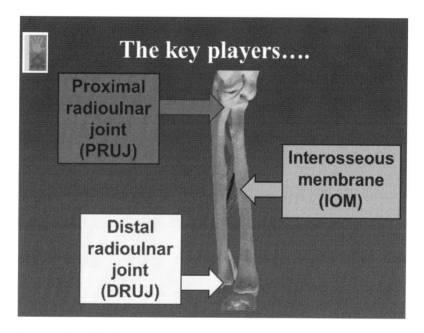

Picture 91: Slide2

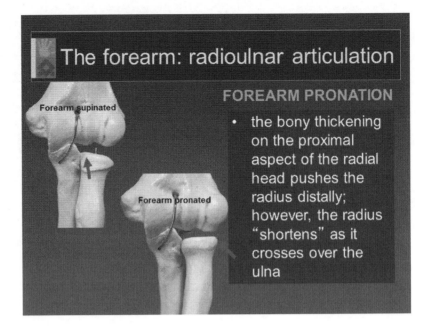

Picture 92: Slide3

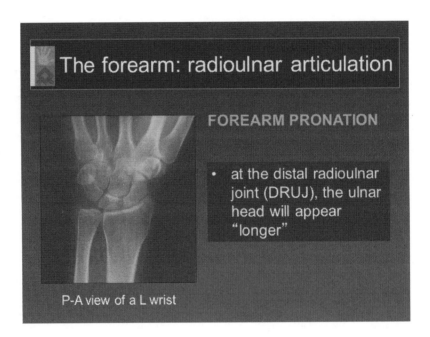

Picture 93: Slide4

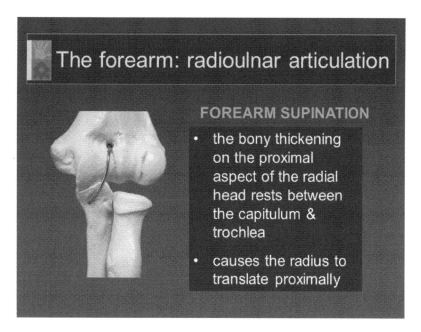

Picture 94: Slide5

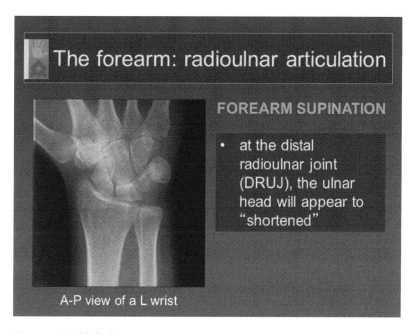

Picture 95: Slide6

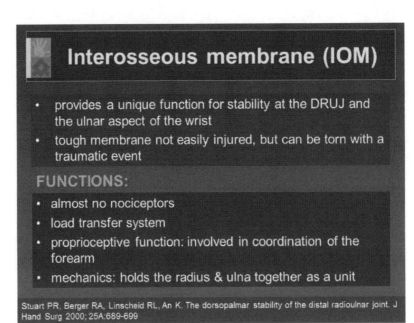

Picture 96: Slide7

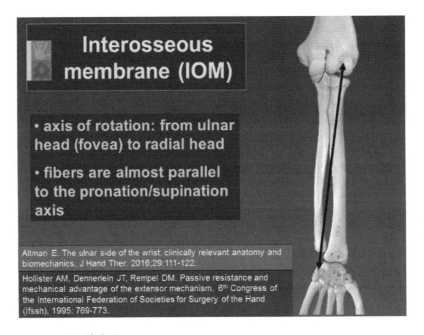

Picture 97: Slide8

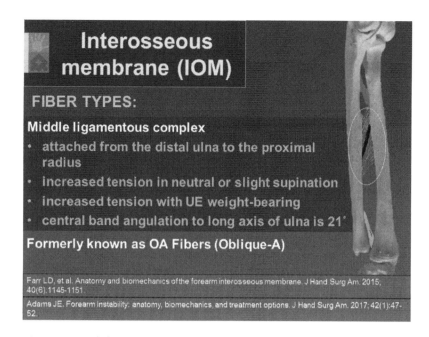

Picture 98: Slide9

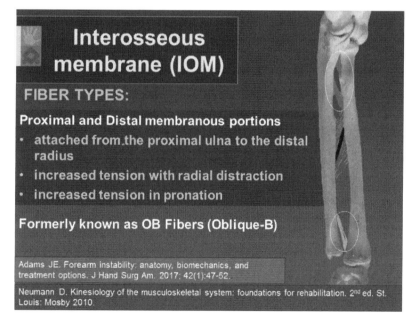

Picture 99: Slide10

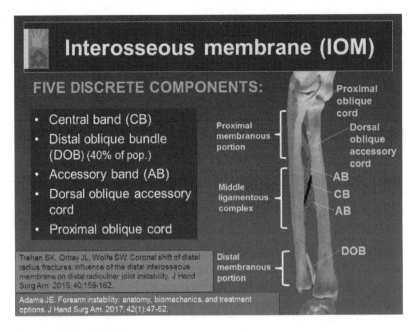

Picture 100: Slide11

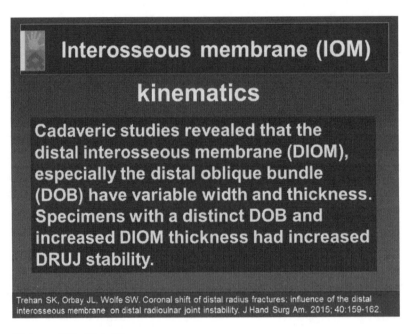

Picture 101: Slide12

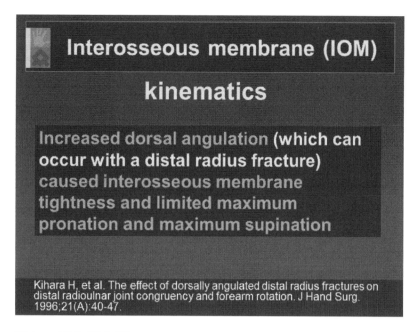

Picture 102: Slide13

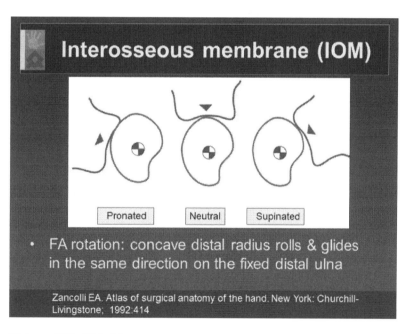

Picture 103: Slide14

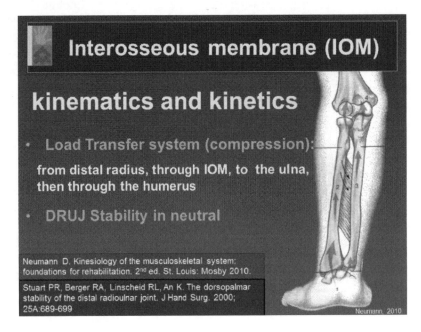

Picture 104: Slide15

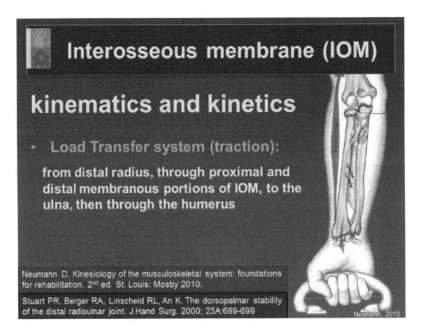

Picture 105: Slide16

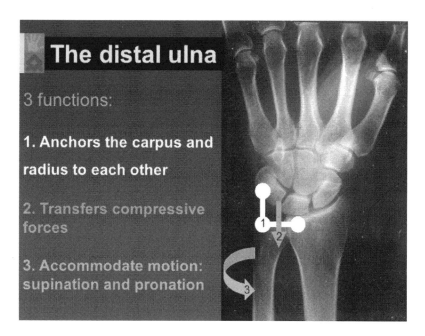

Picture 106: Slide17

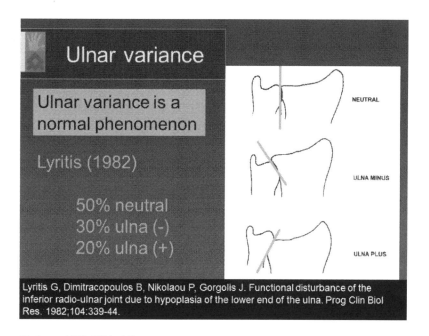

Picture 107: Slide18

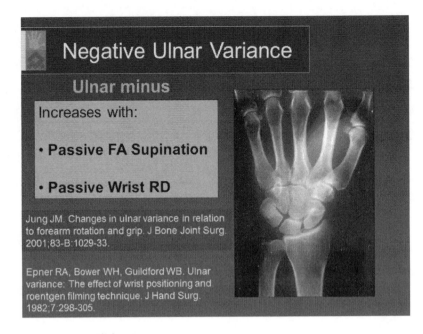

Picture 108: Slide19

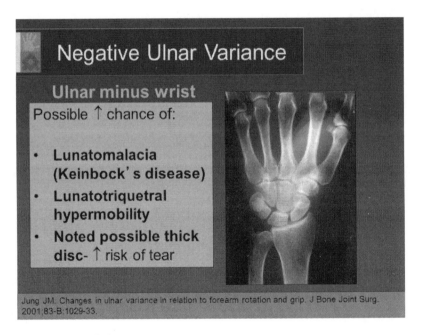

Picture 109: Slide20

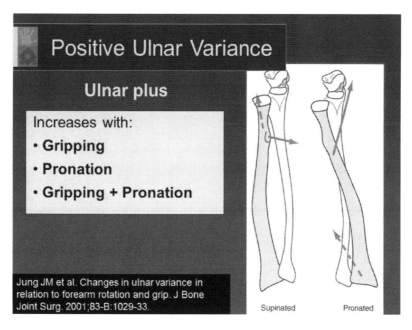

Picture 110: Slide21

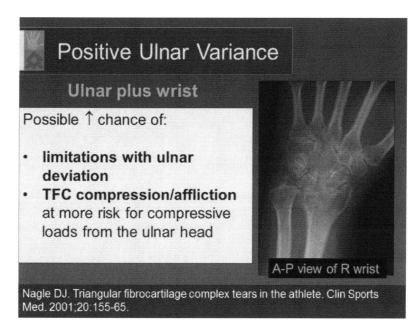

Picture 111: Slide22

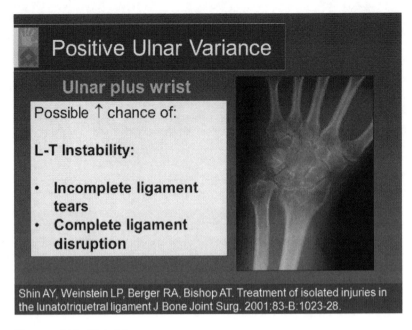

Picture 112: Slide23

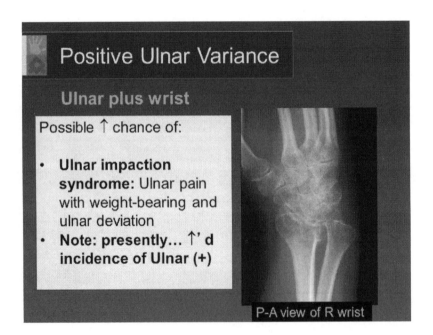

Picture 113: Slide24

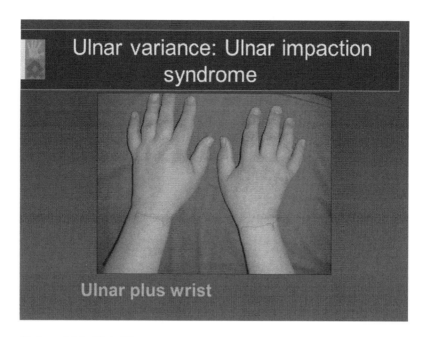

Picture 114: Slide25

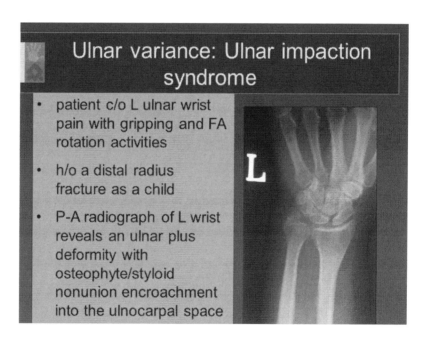

Picture 115: Slide26

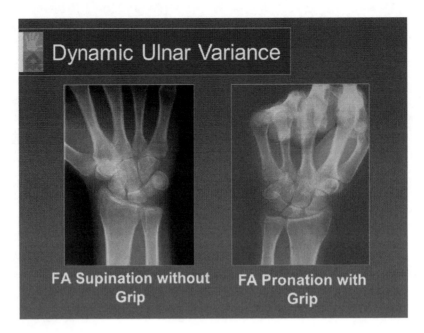

Picture 116: Slide27

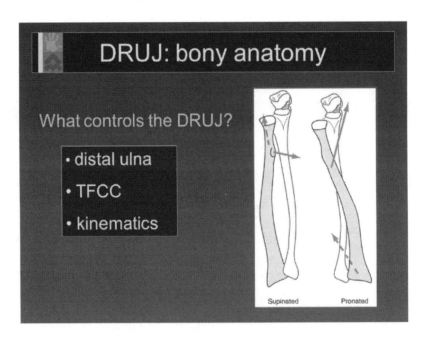

Picture 117: Slide28

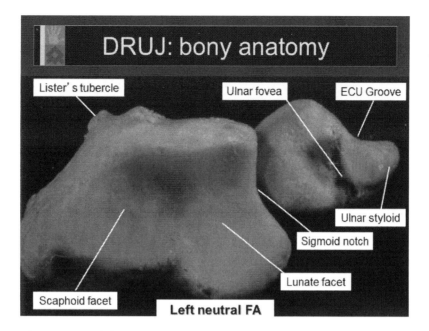

Picture 118: Slide29

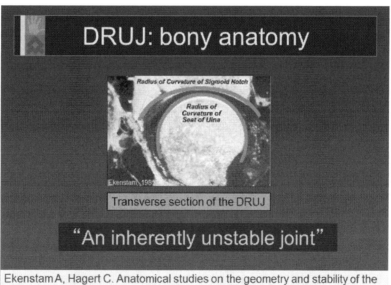

Picture 119: Slide30

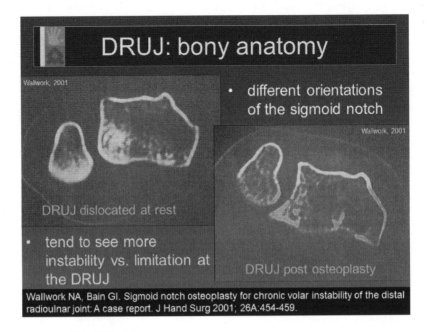

Picture 120: Slide31

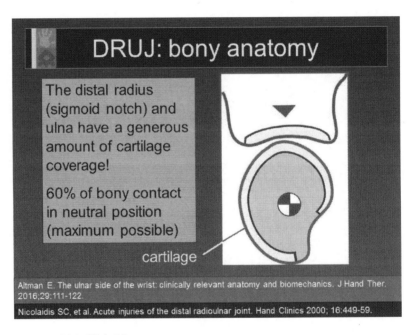

Picture 121: Slide32

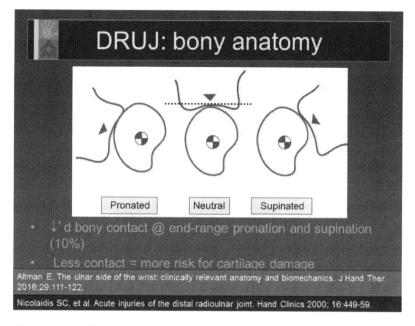

Picture 122: Slide33

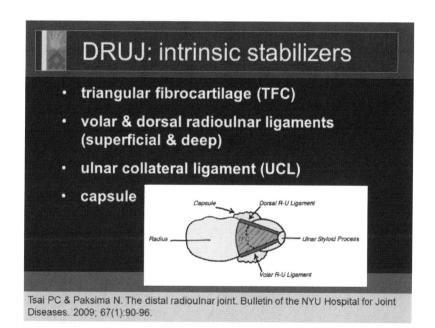

Picture 123: Slide34

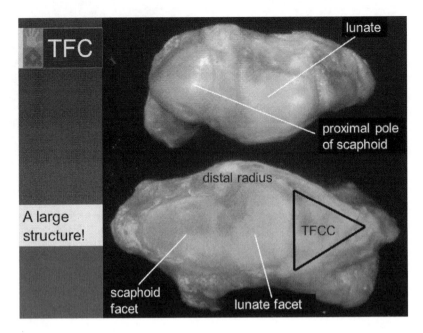

Picture 124: Slide35

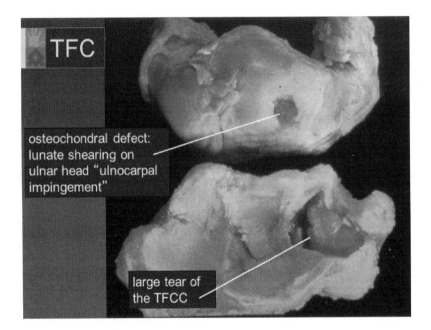

Picture 125: Slide36

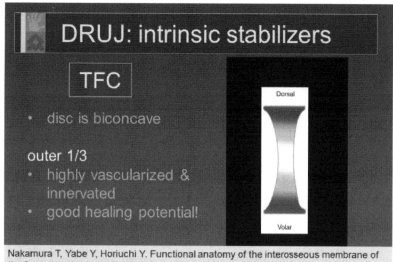

Picture 126: Slide37

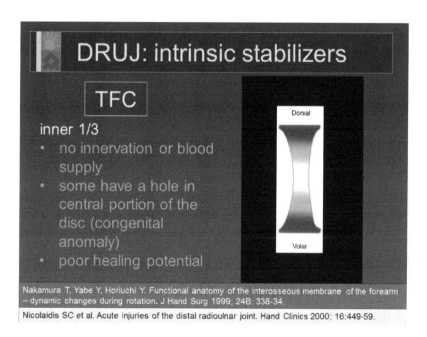

Picture 127: Slide38

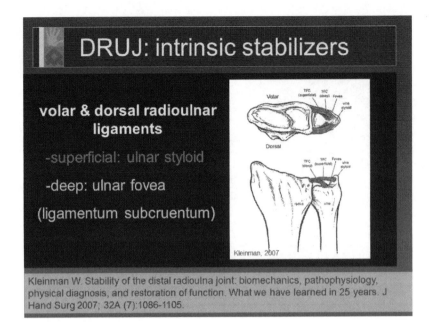

Picture 128: Slide39

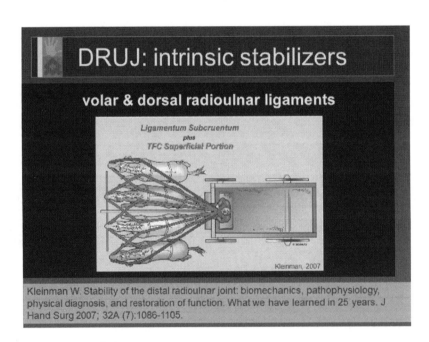

Picture 129: Slide40

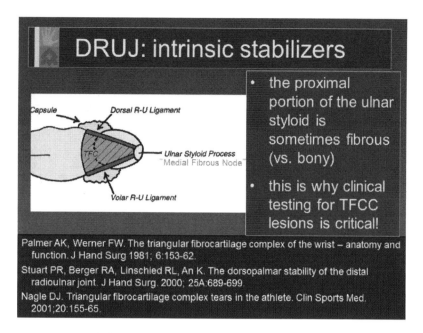

Picture 130: Slide41

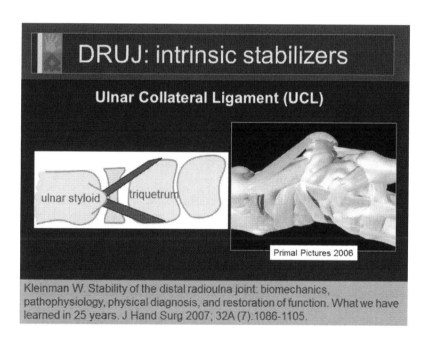

Picture 131: Slide42

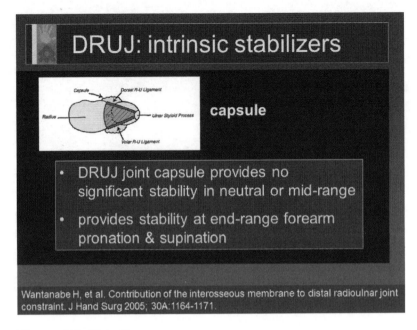

Picture 132: Slide43

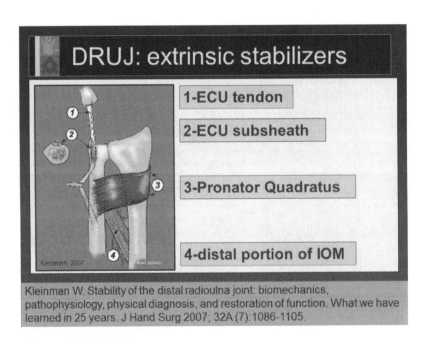

Picture 133: Slide44

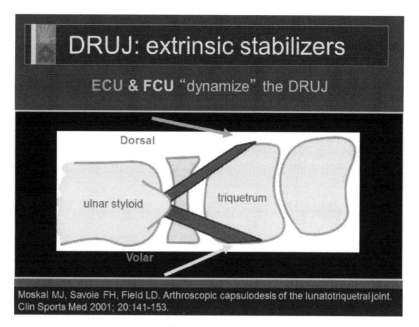

Picture 134: Slide45

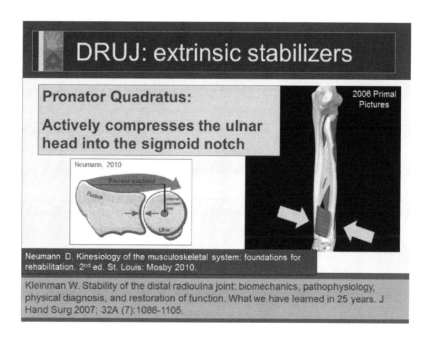

Picture 135: Slide46

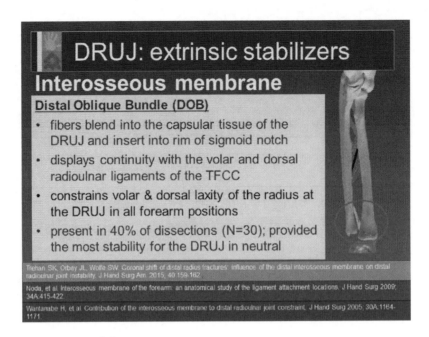

Picture 136: Slide47

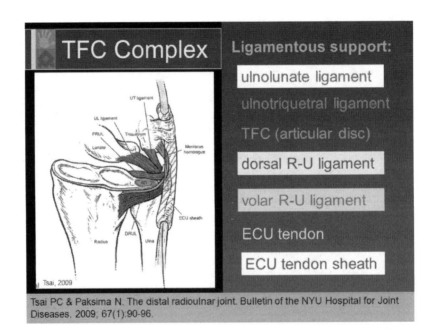

Picture 137: Slide48

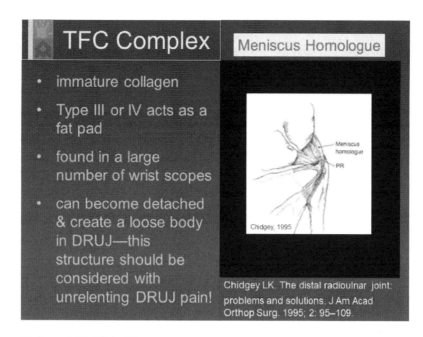

Picture 138: Slide49

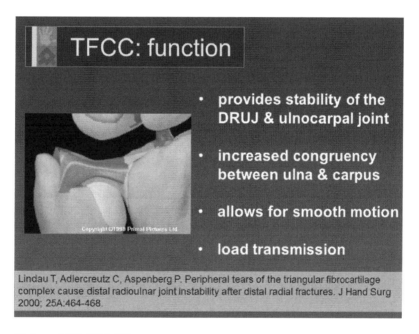

Picture 139: Slide50

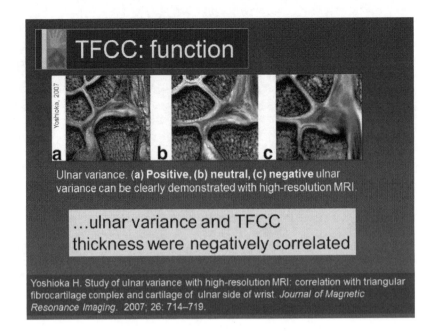

TFCC: function

Ulnar variance. (a) **Positive**, (b) **neutral**, (c) **negative** ulnar variance can be clearly demonstrated with high-resolution MRI.

...ulnar variance and TFCC thickness were negatively correlated

Yoshioka H. Study of ulnar variance with high-resolution MRI: correlation with triangular fibrocartilage complex and cartilage of ulnar side of wrist. *Journal of Magnetic Resonance Imaging.* 2007; 26: 714–719.

Picture 140: Slide51

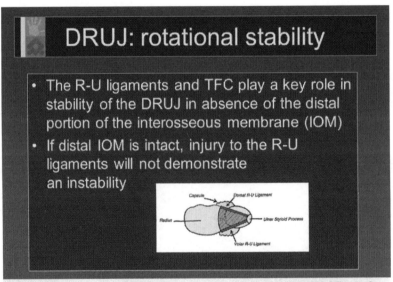

DRUJ: rotational stability

- The R-U ligaments and TFC play a key role in stability of the DRUJ in absence of the distal portion of the interosseous membrane (IOM)
- If distal IOM is intact, injury to the R-U ligaments will not demonstrate an instability

Gofton WT, Gordon KD, Dunning CD, Johnson JA, King GJ. Soft-tissue stabilizers of the distal radioulnar joint: an in vitro kinematic study. J Hand Surg. 2004; 25(3):423-431.

Picture 141: Slide52

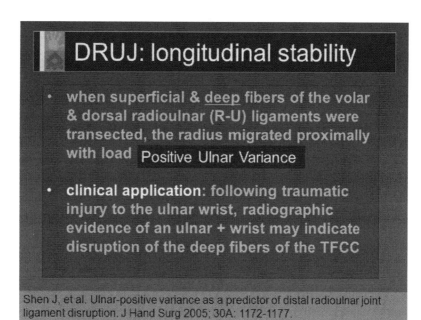

Picture 142: Slide53

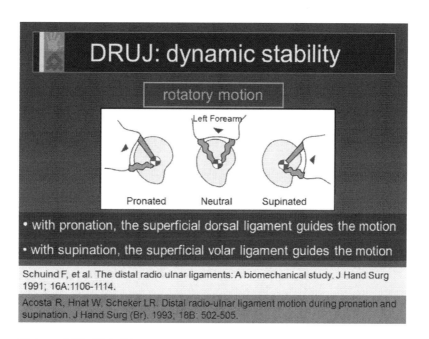

Picture 143: Slide54

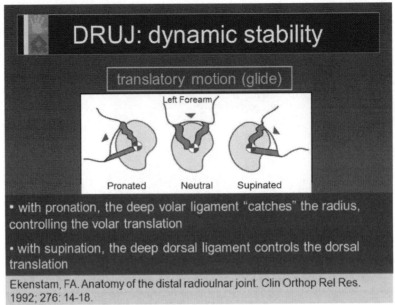

Picture 144: Slide55

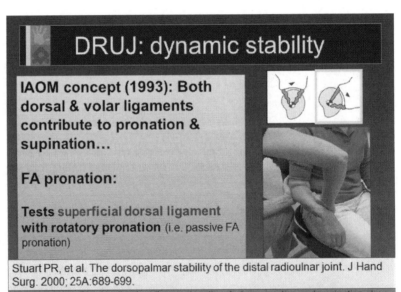

Picture 145: Slide56

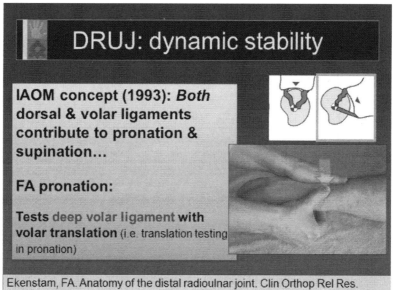

Picture 146: Slide57

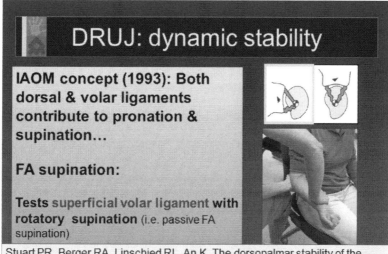

Picture 147: Slide58

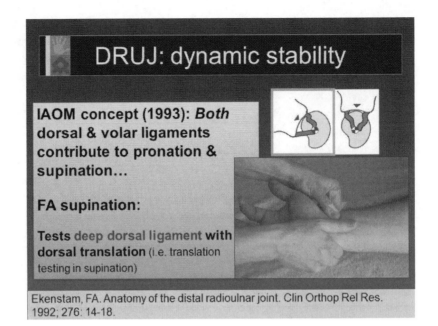

Picture 148: Slide59

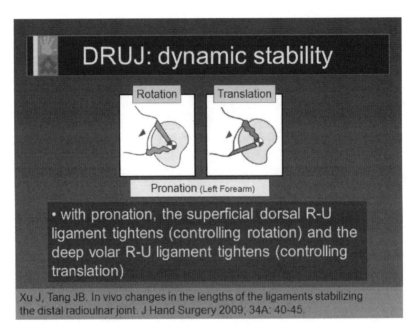

Picture 149: Slide60

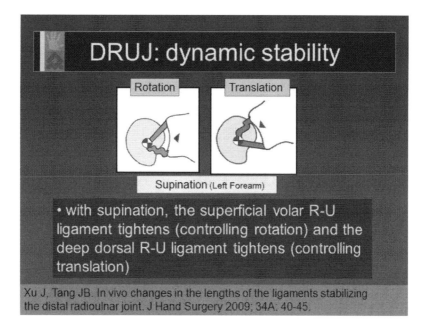

Picture 150: Slide61

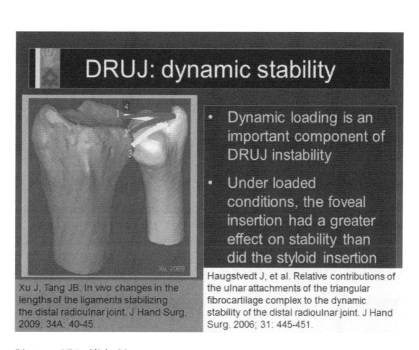

Picture 151: Slide62

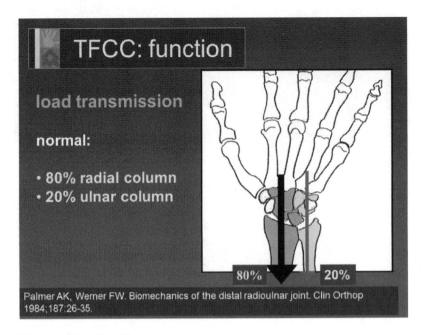

Picture 152: Slide63

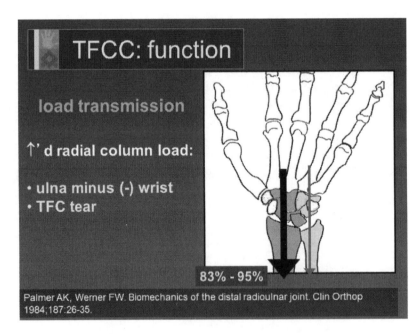

Picture 153: Slide64

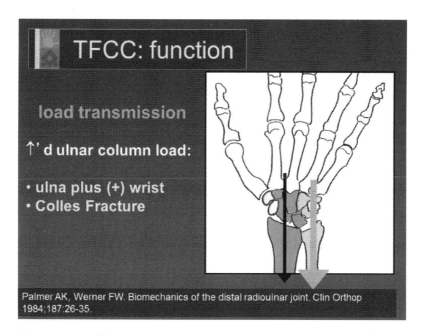

Picture 154: Slide65

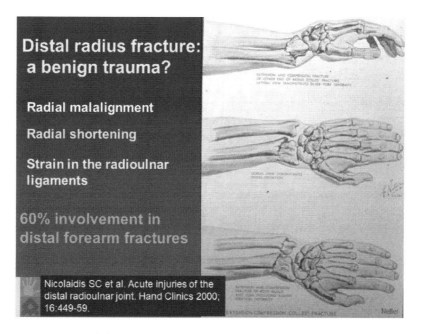

Picture 155: Slide66

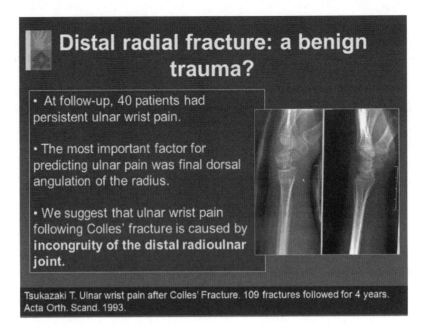

Picture 156: Slide67

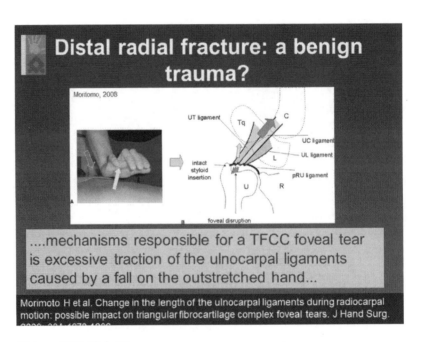

Picture 157: Slide68

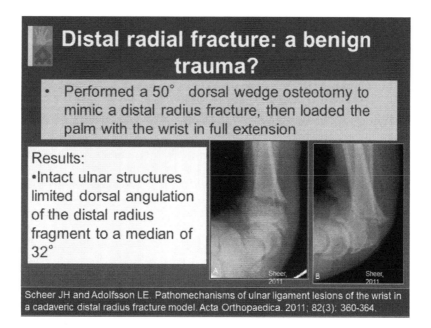

Picture 158: Slide69

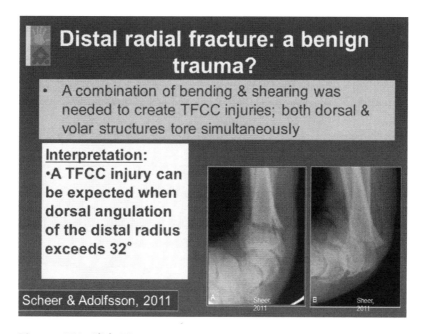

Picture 159: Slide70

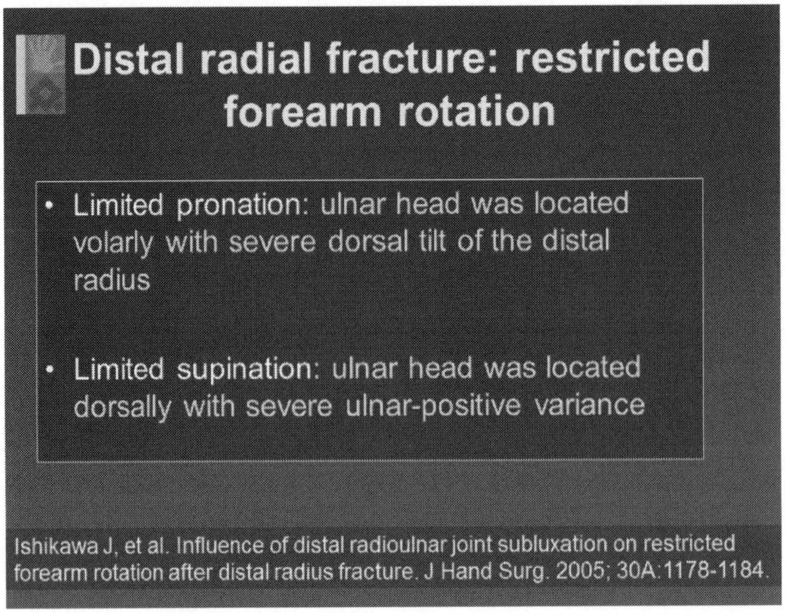

Distal radial fracture: restricted forearm rotation

- Limited pronation: ulnar head was located volarly with severe dorsal tilt of the distal radius

- Limited supination: ulnar head was located dorsally with severe ulnar-positive variance

Ishikawa J, et al. Influence of distal radioulnar joint subluxation on restricted forearm rotation after distal radius fracture. J Hand Surg. 2005; 30A:1178-1184.

Picture 160: Slide71

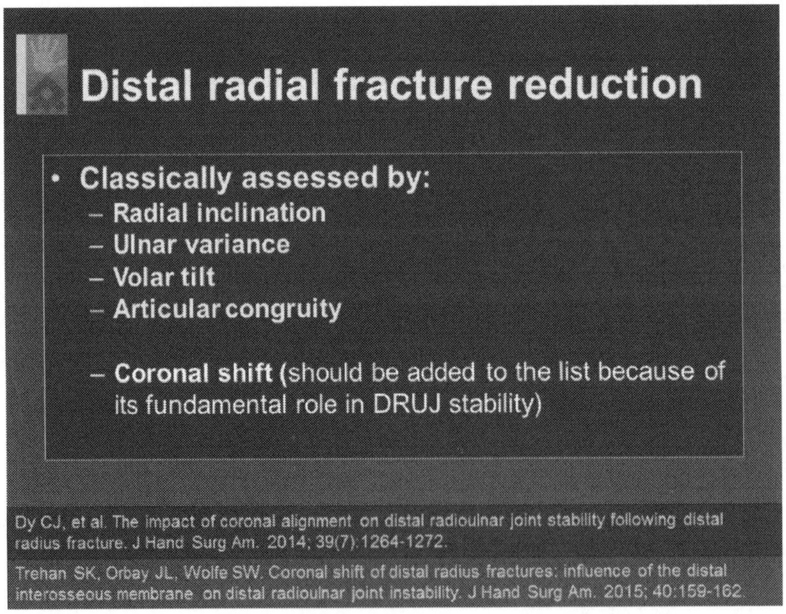

Distal radial fracture reduction

- **Classically assessed by:**
  - **Radial inclination**
  - **Ulnar variance**
  - **Volar tilt**
  - **Articular congruity**

  - **Coronal shift** (should be added to the list because of its fundamental role in DRUJ stability)

Dy CJ, et al. The impact of coronal alignment on distal radioulnar joint stability following distal radius fracture. J Hand Surg Am. 2014; 39(7):1264-1272.

Trehan SK, Orbay JL, Wolfe SW. Coronal shift of distal radius fractures: influence of the distal interosseous membrane on distal radioulnar joint instability. J Hand Surg Am. 2015; 40:159-162.

Picture 161: Slide72

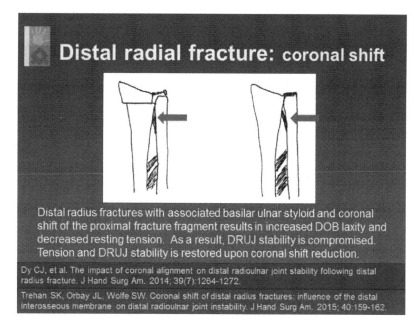

Distal radial fracture: coronal shift

Distal radius fractures with associated basilar ulnar styloid and coronal shift of the proximal fracture fragment results in increased DOB laxity and decreased resting tension. As a result, DRUJ stability is compromised. Tension and DRUJ stability is restored upon coronal shift reduction.

Dy CJ, et al. The impact of coronal alignment on distal radioulnar joint stability following distal radius fracture. J Hand Surg Am. 2014; 39(7):1264-1272.

Trehan SK, Orbay JL, Wolfe SW. Coronal shift of distal radius fractures: influence of the distal interosseous membrane on distal radioulnar joint instability. J Hand Surg Am. 2015; 40:159-162.

Picture 162: Slide73

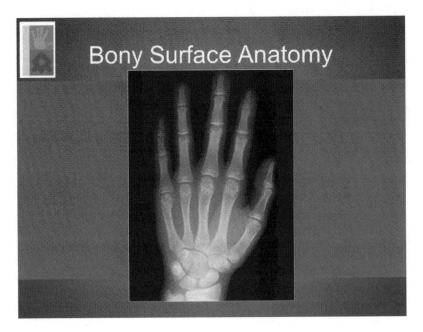

Picture 163: Slide1

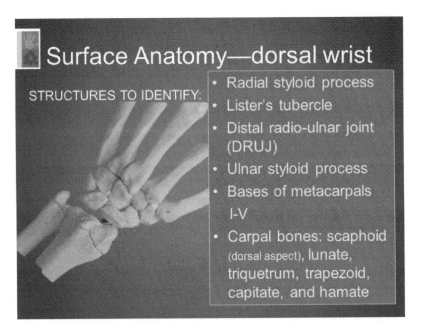

Picture 164: Slide2

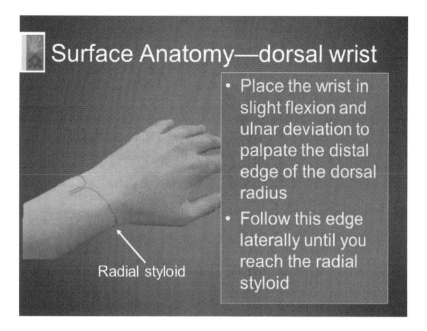

Picture 165: Slide3

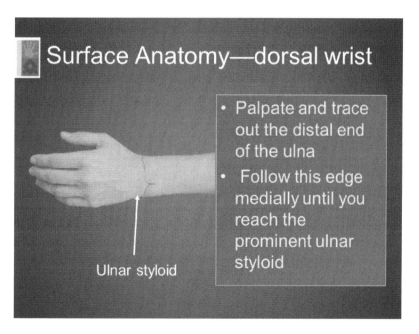

Picture 166: Slide4

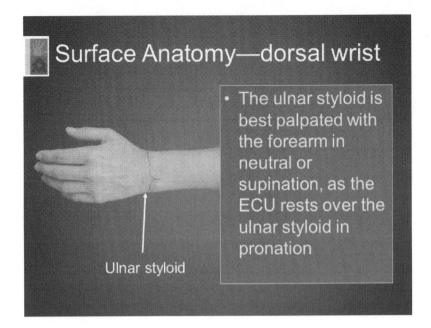

Picture 167: Slide5

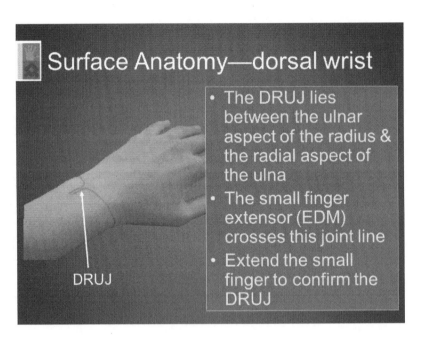

Picture 168: Slide6

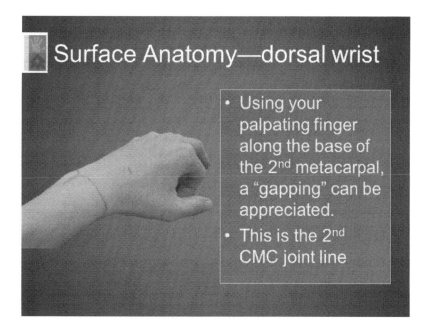

Picture 169: Slide7

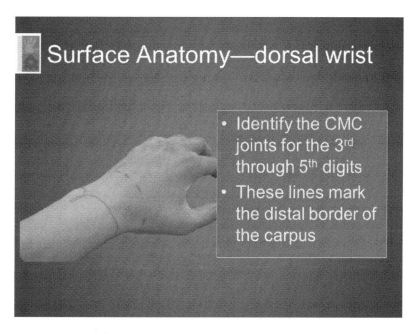

Picture 170: Slide8

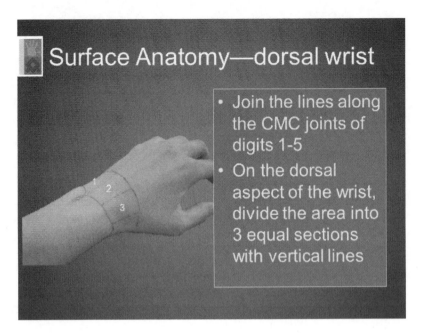

Picture 171: Slide9

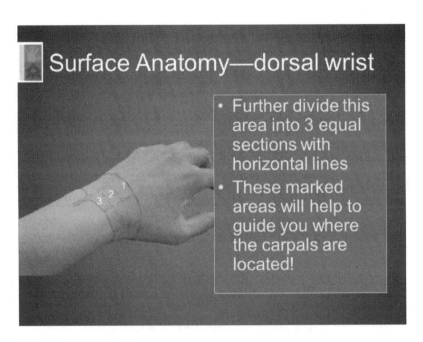

Picture 172: Slide10

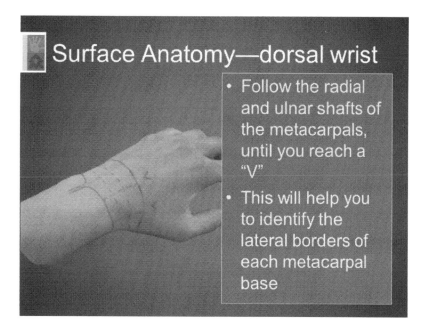

Picture 173: Slide11

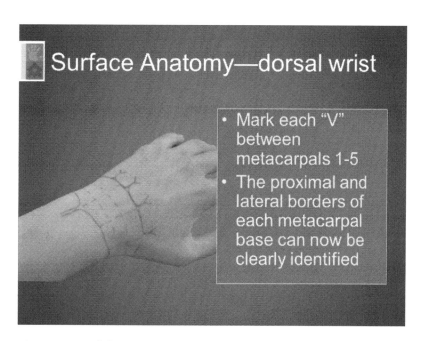

Picture 174: Slide12

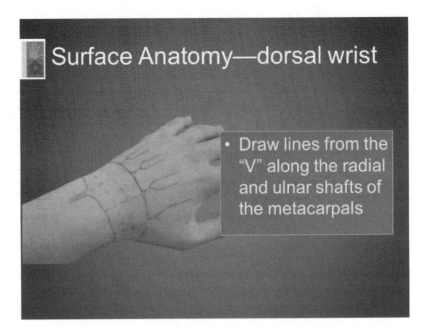

Picture 175: Slide13

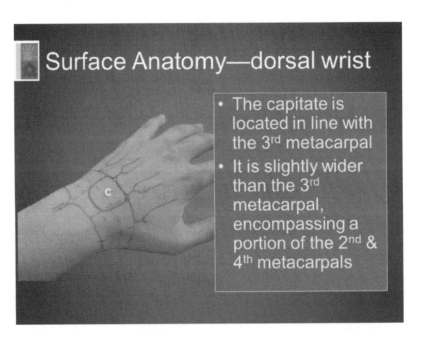

Picture 176: Slide14

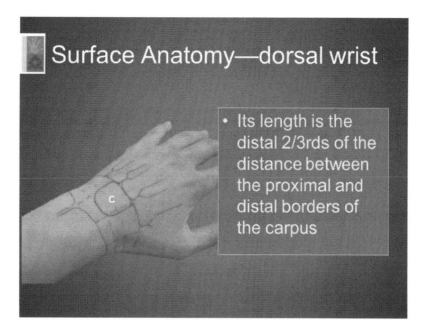

Picture 177: Slide15

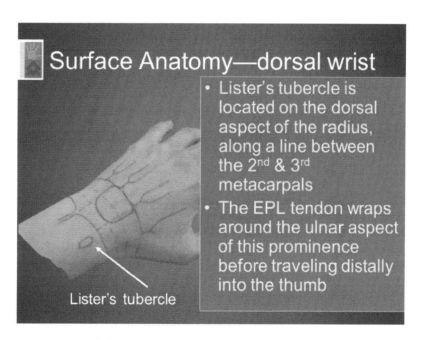

Picture 178: Slide16

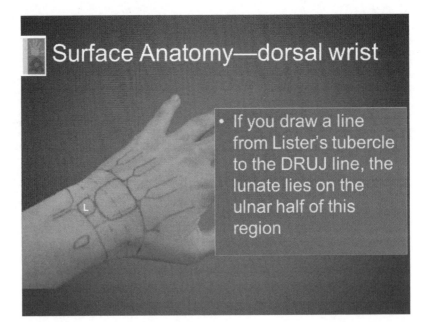

Picture 179: Slide17

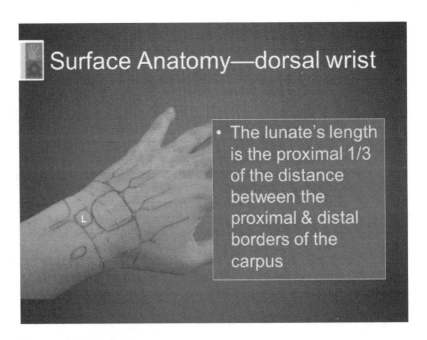

Picture 180: Slide18

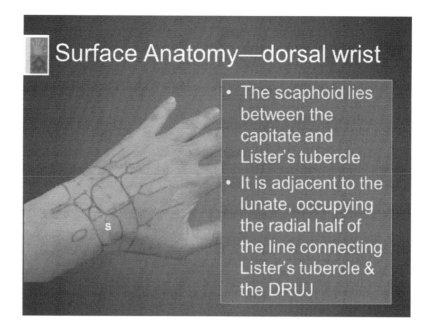

Picture 181: Slide19

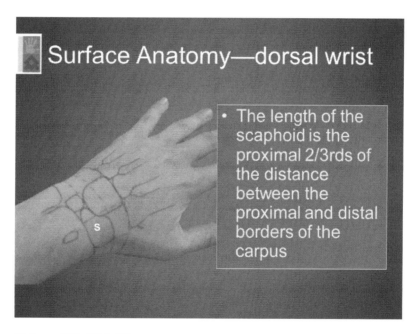

Picture 182: Slide20

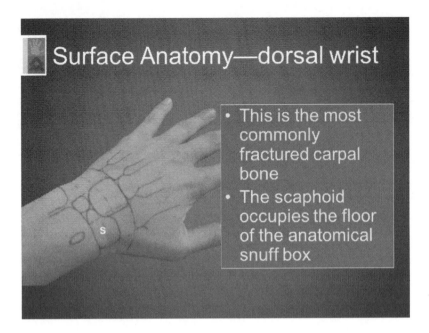

Picture 183: Slide21

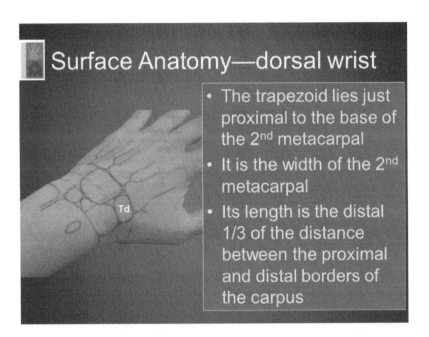

Picture 184: Slide22

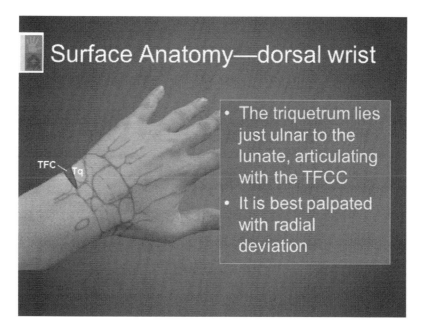

Picture 185: Slide23

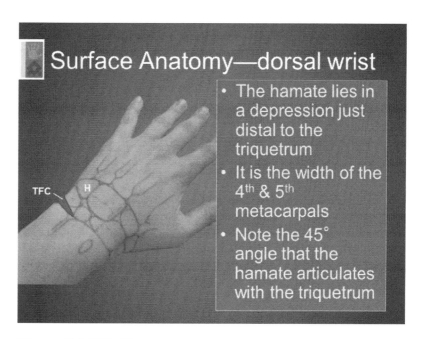

Picture 186: Slide24

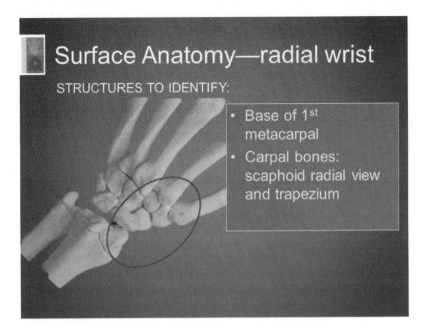

Picture 187: Slide25

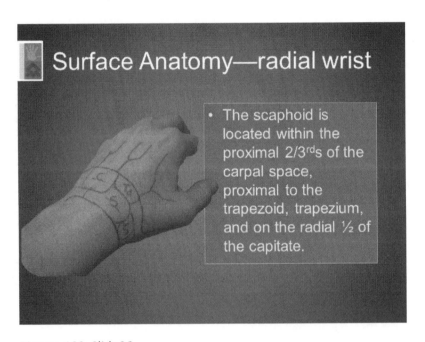

Picture 188: Slide26

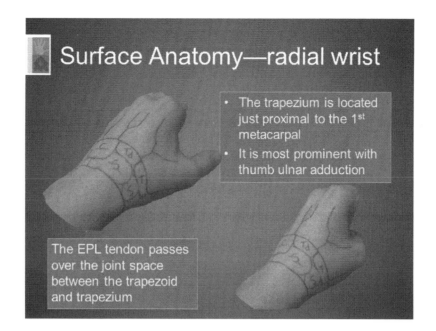

Picture 189: Slide27

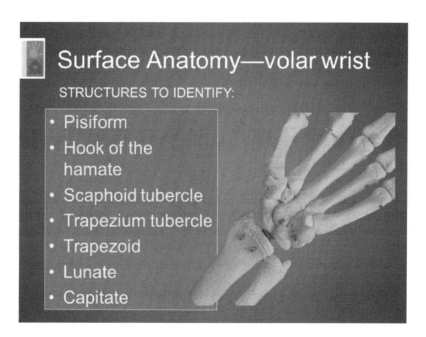

Picture 190: Slide28

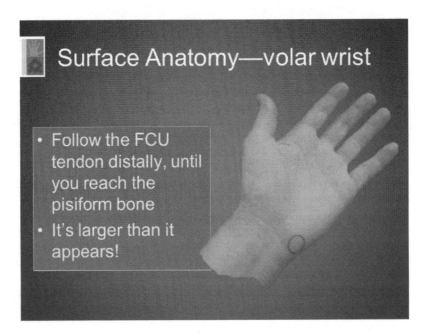

Picture 191: Slide29

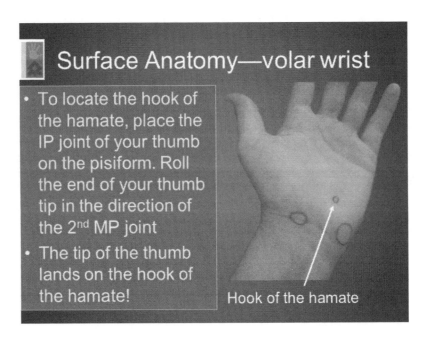

Picture 192: Slide30

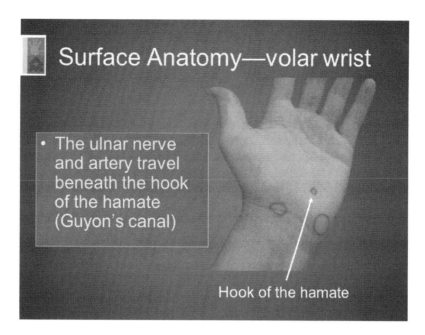

Picture 193: Slide31

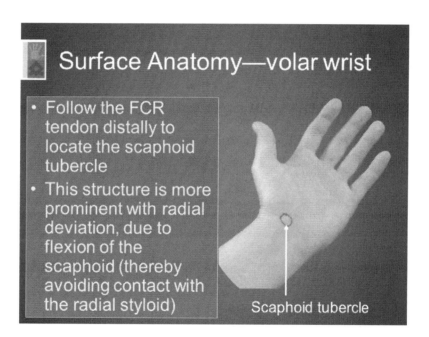

Picture 194: Slide32

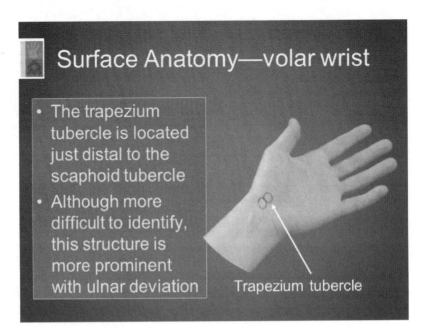

Surface Anatomy—volar wrist

- The trapezium tubercle is located just distal to the scaphoid tubercle
- Although more difficult to identify, this structure is more prominent with ulnar deviation

Trapezium tubercle

Picture 195: Slide33

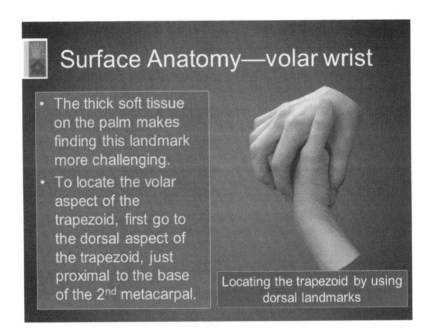

Surface Anatomy—volar wrist

- The thick soft tissue on the palm makes finding this landmark more challenging.
- To locate the volar aspect of the trapezoid, first go to the dorsal aspect of the trapezoid, just proximal to the base of the 2nd metacarpal.

Locating the trapezoid by using dorsal landmarks

Picture 196: Slide34

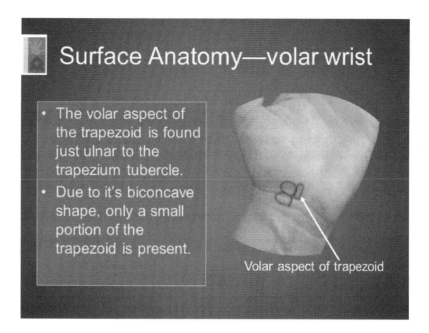

Picture 197: Slide35

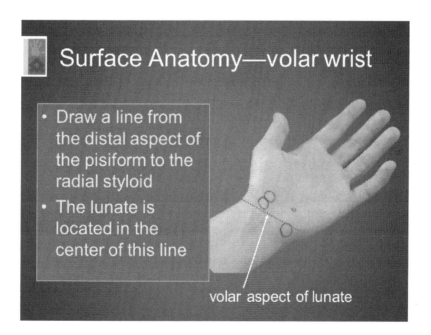

Picture 198: Slide36

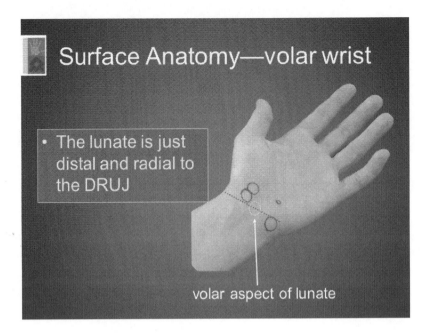

Picture 199: Slide37

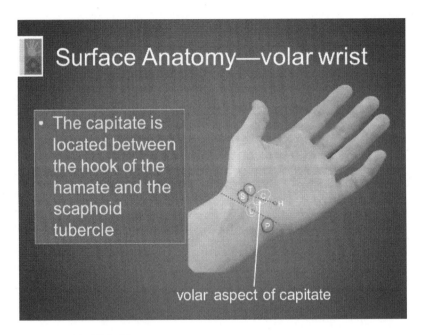

Picture 200: Slide38

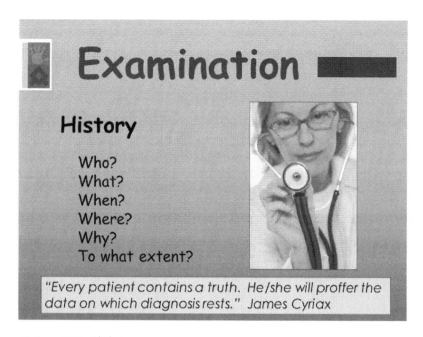

Picture 201: Slide1

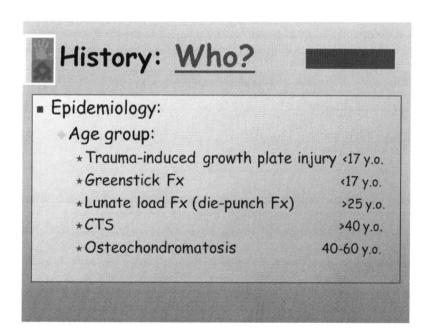

Picture 202: Slide2

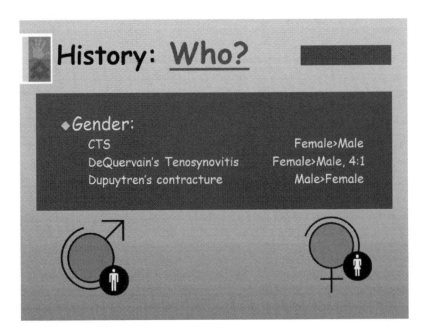

Picture 203: Slide3

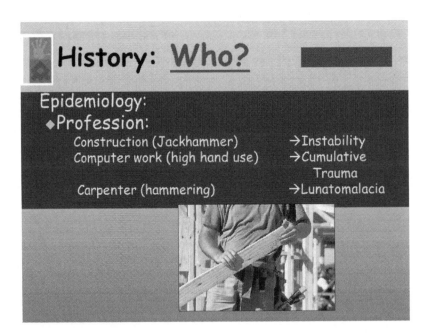

Picture 204: Slide4

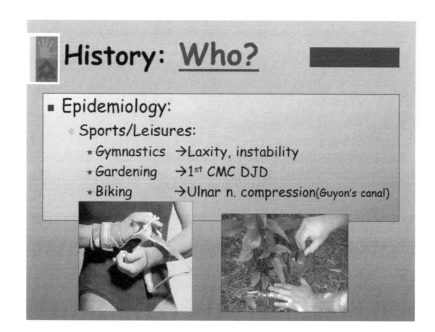

Picture 205: Slide5

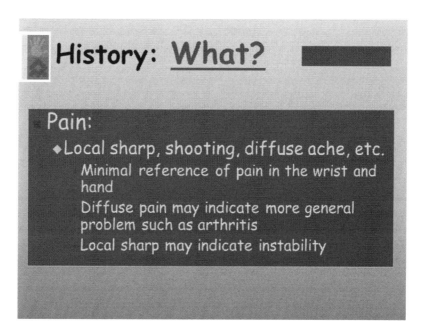

Picture 206: Slide6

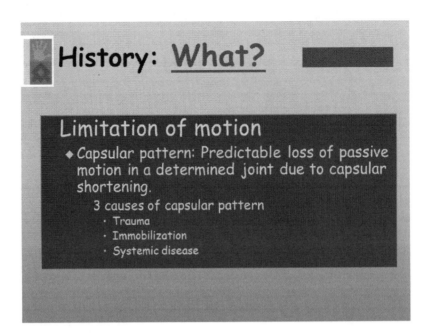

Picture 207: Slide7

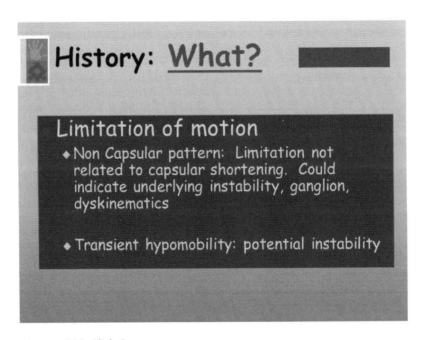

Picture 208: Slide8

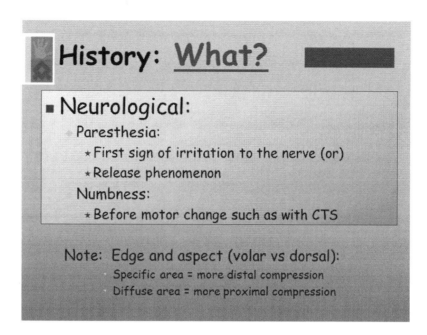

Picture 209: Slide9

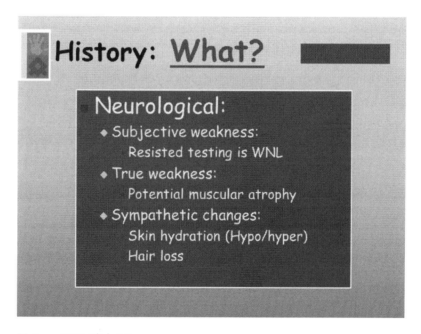

Picture 210: Slide10

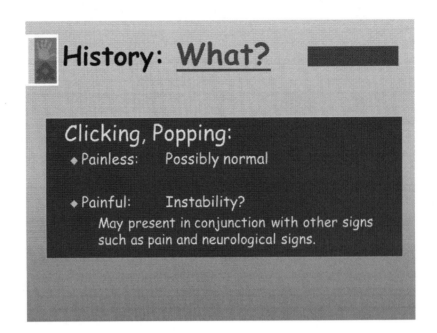

Picture 211: Slide11

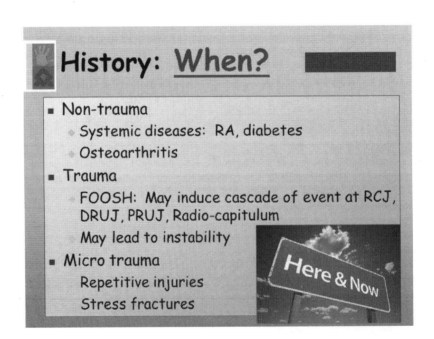

Picture 212: Slide12

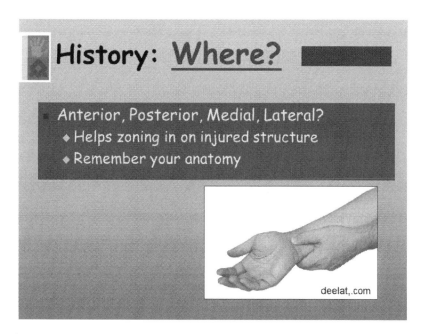

Picture 213: Slide13

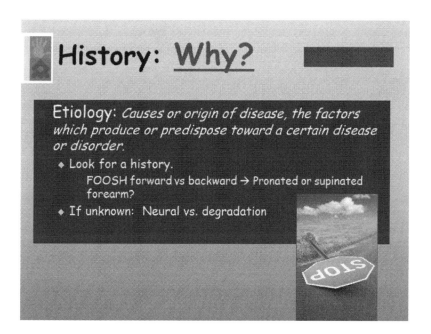

Picture 214: Slide14

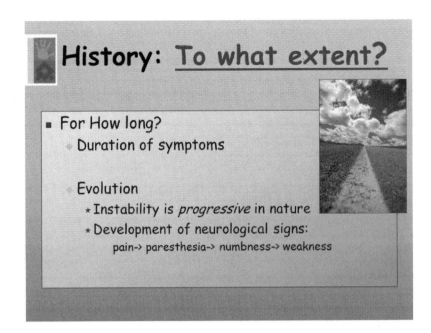

Picture 215: Slide15

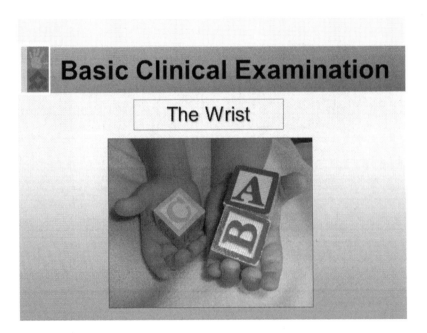

Picture 216: Slide16

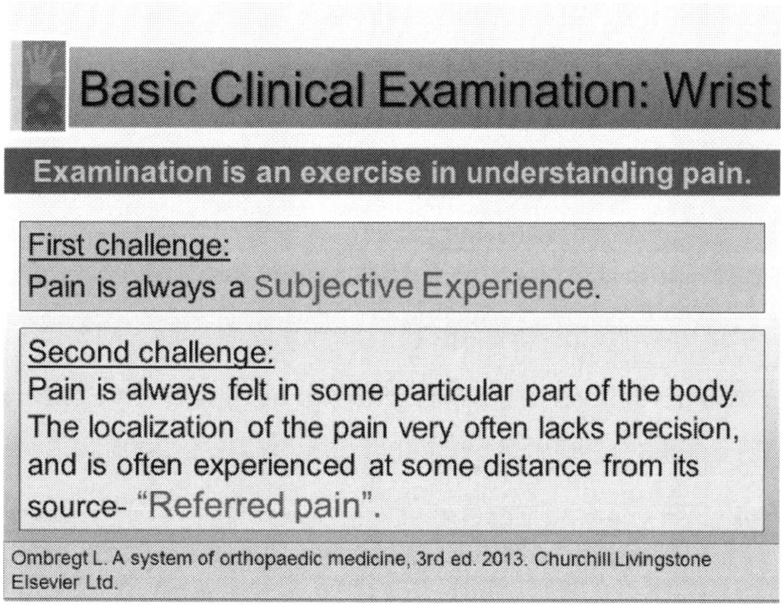

Basic Clinical Examination: Wrist

Examination is an exercise in understanding pain.

First challenge:
Pain is always a Subjective Experience.

Second challenge:
Pain is always felt in some particular part of the body. The localization of the pain very often lacks precision, and is often experienced at some distance from its source- "Referred pain".

Ombregt L. A system of orthopaedic medicine, 3rd ed. 2013. Churchill Livingstone Elsevier Ltd.

Picture 217: Slide17

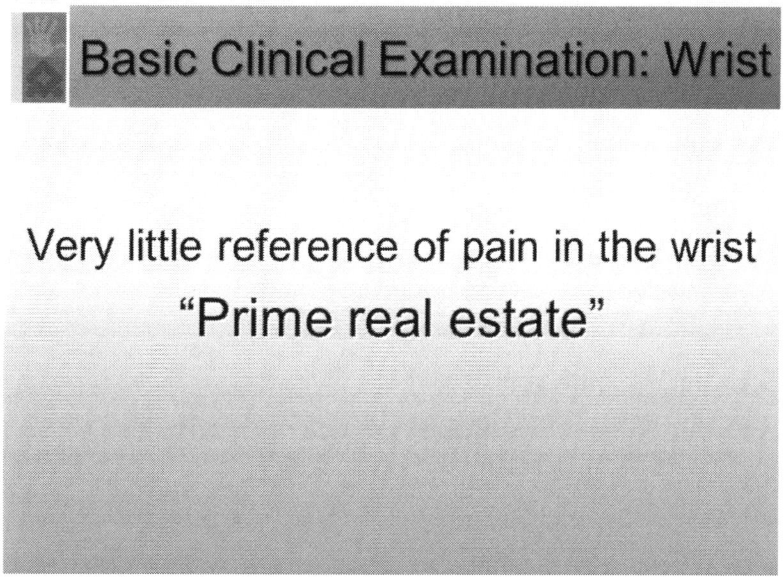

Basic Clinical Examination: Wrist

Very little reference of pain in the wrist
"Prime real estate"

Picture 218: Slide18

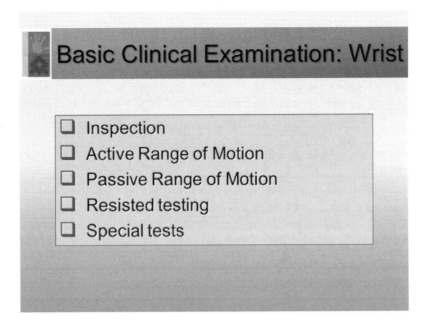

Picture 219: Slide19

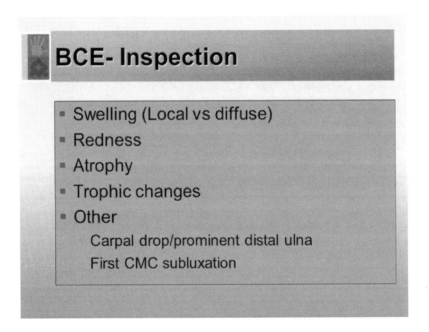

Picture 220: Slide20

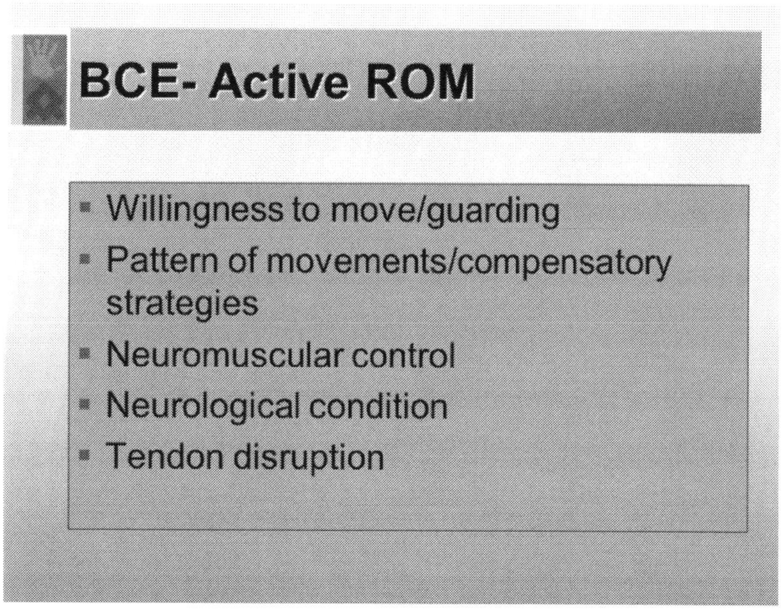

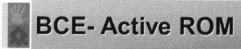

BCE- Active ROM
Willingness to move/guarding
Pattern of movements/compensatory strategies
Neuromuscular control
Neurological condition
Tendon disruption

Picture 221: Slide21

BCE- Active ROM
Active Flexion Recruitment patterns
Initiating motion with finger flexors
Initiating motion with wrist flexors

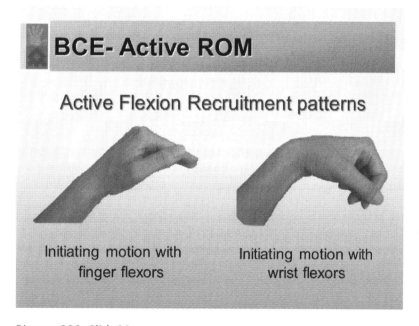

Picture 222: Slide22

BCE- Active ROM
Active Extension Recruitment patterns
Initiating motion with finger extensors
Initiating motion with wrist extensors

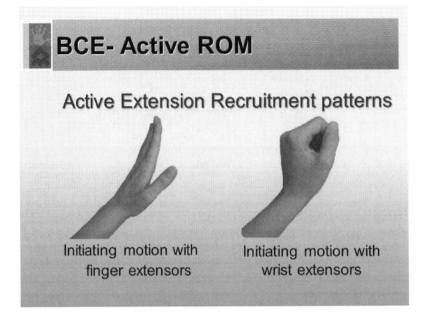

Picture 223: Slide23

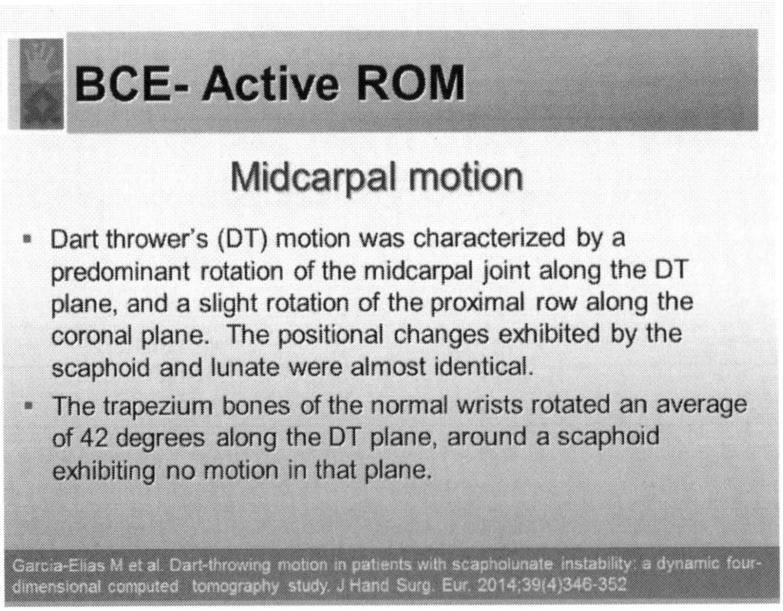

BCE- Active ROM
Midcarpal motion
Dart thrower's (DT) motion was characterized by a predominant rotation of the midcarpal joint along the DT plane, and a slight rotation of the proximal row along the coronal plane. The positional changes exhibited by the scaphoid and lunate were almost identical.
The trapezium bones of the normal wrists rotated an average of 42 degrees along the DT plane, around a scaphoid exhibiting no motion in that plane.
Garcia-Elias M et al. Dart-throwing motion in patients with scapholunate instability: a dynamic four-dimensional computed tomography study. J Hand Surg. Eur. 2014;39(4)346-352

Picture 224: Slide24

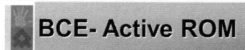

BCE- Active ROM

Midcarpal motion

Cadaver demonstration showed:

- Functional DTM total range of motion: 178°
- Flexion-Extension total range of motion: 129°

Difference of 49°

A significant contribution to function

Moritomo H et al. IFSSH 2013 committee's report of wrist dart-throwing motion. J Hand Surg. Am. 2014; 39(7): 1433-1439.

Picture 225: Slide25

BCE- Active ROM

Screening of Midcarpal motion

Measuring coupled wrist motion clinically has presented unique challenges unlike the goniometric measurement of the conventional orthogonal planes of flexion-extension and radial and ulnar deviation which has been demonstrated to be accurate and reproducible within 10°.

Moritomo H et al. IFSSH 2013 committee's report of wrist dart-throwing motion. J Hand Surg. Am. 2014; 39(7): 1433-1439.

Picture 226: Slide26

BCE- Active ROM

Proposed screening of Midcarpal motion:

Simultaneous bilateral comparison of functional DTM (~45 degrees of forearm pronation)

Picture 227: Slide27

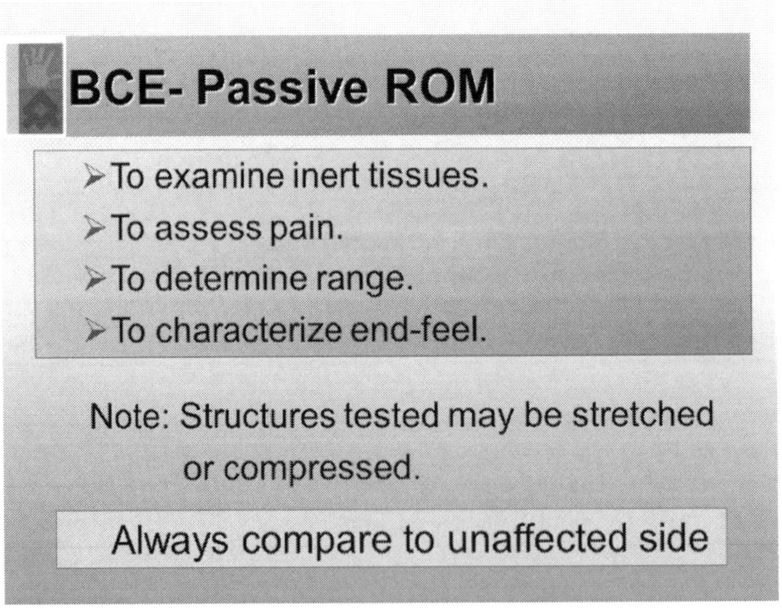

BCE- Passive ROM

➢ To examine inert tissues.
➢ To assess pain.
➢ To determine range.
➢ To characterize end-feel.

Note: Structures tested may be stretched or compressed.

Always compare to unaffected side

Picture 228: Slide28

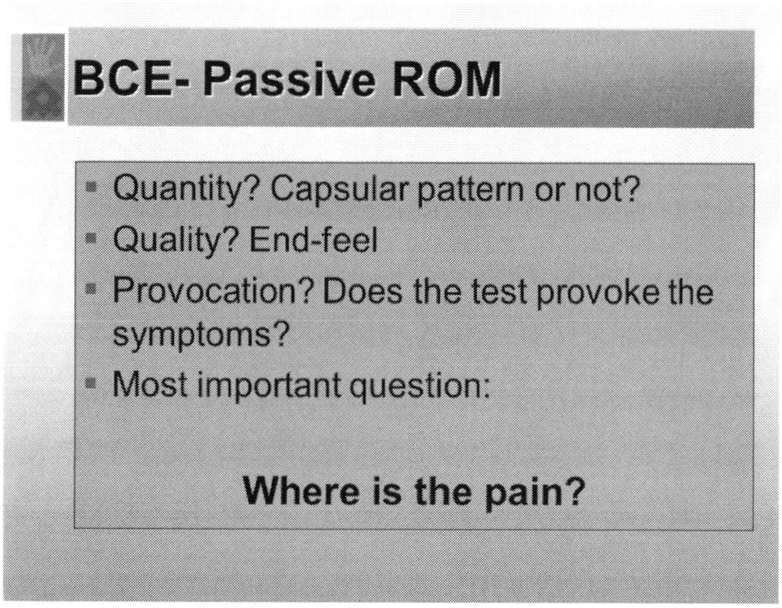

BCE- Passive ROM

- Quantity? Capsular pattern or not?
- Quality? End-feel
- Provocation? Does the test provoke the symptoms?
- Most important question:

Where is the pain?

Picture 229: Slide29

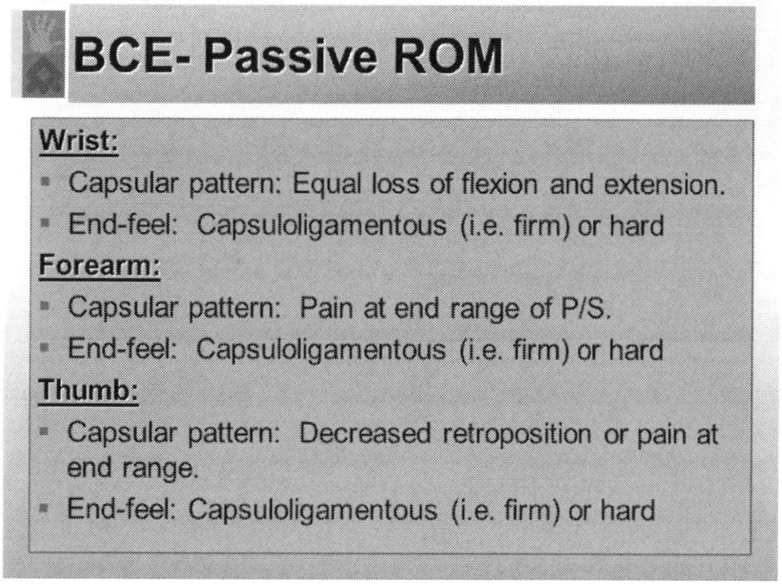

BCE- Passive ROM

Wrist:
- Capsular pattern: Equal loss of flexion and extension.
- End-feel: Capsuloligamentous (i.e. firm) or hard

Forearm:
- Capsular pattern: Pain at end range of P/S.
- End-feel: Capsuloligamentous (i.e. firm) or hard

Thumb:
- Capsular pattern: Decreased retroposition or pain at end range.
- End-feel: Capsuloligamentous (i.e. firm) or hard

Picture 230: Slide30

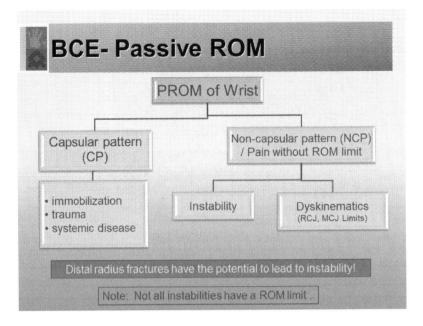

Picture 231: Slide31

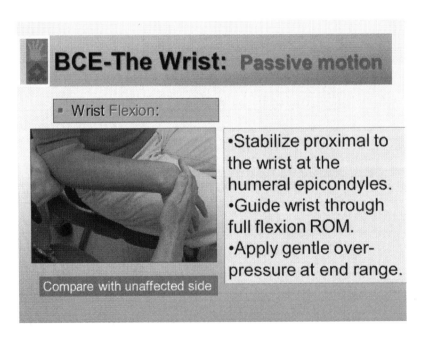

Picture 232: Slide32

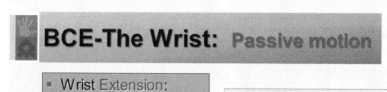

BCE-The Wrist: Passive motion

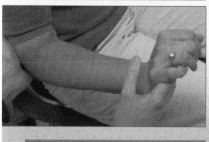

■ Wrist Extension:

Compare with unaffected side

•Stabilize proximal to the wrist at the humeral epicondyles.
•Guide wrist through full extension ROM.
•Apply gentle over-pressure at end range.

Picture 233: Slide33

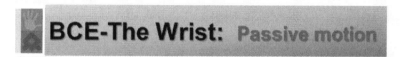

BCE-The Wrist: Passive motion

■ Wrist Radial Deviation: In neutral

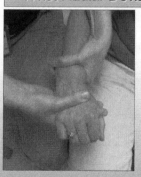

•Stabilize forearm proximal to the RCJ.
•Guide wrist through full range of passive radial deviation in a neutral plane.
•Apply gentle overpressure at end range.

Compare with unaffected side

Picture 234: Slide34

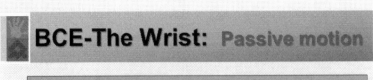

BCE-The Wrist: Passive motion

■ Wrist Radial Deviation: In slight extension

Compare with unaffected side

•Stabilize forearm proximal to the RCJ.
•Guide wrist through full range of passive radial deviation in slight extension.
•Apply gentle over-pressure at end range.

Picture 235: Slide35

BCE-The Wrist: Passive motion

■ Wrist Radial Deviation: In slight flexion

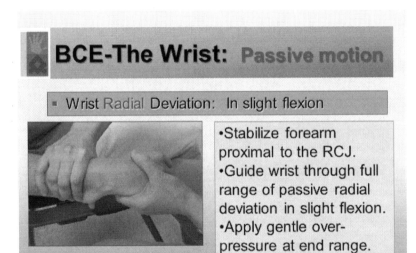

Compare with unaffected side

•Stabilize forearm proximal to the RCJ.
•Guide wrist through full range of passive radial deviation in slight flexion.
•Apply gentle over-pressure at end range.

Picture 236: Slide36

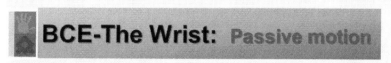

BCE-The Wrist: Passive motion

- Wrist Ulnar Deviation: In neutral

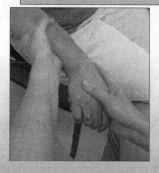

- Stabilize forearm proximal to the RCJ.
- Guide wrist through full range of passive ulnar deviation in a neutral plane.
- Apply gentle overpressure at end range.

Compare with unaffected side

Picture 237: Slide37

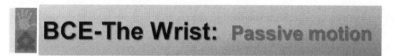

BCE-The Wrist: Passive motion

- Wrist Ulnar Deviation: In slight extension

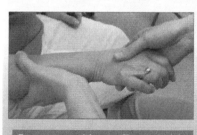

Compare with unaffected side

- Stabilize forearm proximal to the RCJ.
- Guide wrist through full range of passive ulnar deviation in slight extension.
- Apply gentle over-pressure at end range.

Picture 238: Slide38

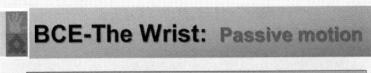

BCE-The Wrist: Passive motion

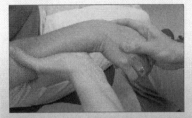

- Wrist Ulnar Deviation: In slight flexion

Compare with unaffected side

•Stabilize forearm proximal to the RCJ.
•Guide wrist through full range of passive ulnar deviation in slight flexion.
•Apply gentle overpressure at end range.

Picture 239: Slide39

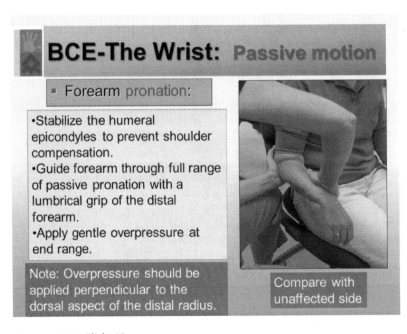

BCE-The Wrist: Passive motion

- Forearm pronation:

•Stabilize the humeral epicondyles to prevent shoulder compensation.
•Guide forearm through full range of passive pronation with a lumbrical grip of the distal forearm.
•Apply gentle overpressure at end range.

Note: Overpressure should be applied perpendicular to the dorsal aspect of the distal radius.

Compare with unaffected side

Picture 240: Slide40

BCE-The Wrist: Passive motion

- Forearm supination:

•Stabilize the humeral epicondyles to prevent shoulder compensation.
•Guide forearm through full range of passive supination with a lumbrical grip of the distal forearm.
•Apply gentle overpressure at end range.

Note: Overpressure should be applied perpendicular to the volar aspect of the distal radius.

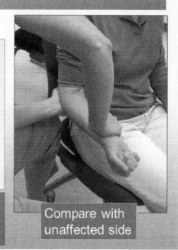

Compare with unaffected side

Picture 241: Slide41

BCE-The Wrist: Passive motion

- Thumb retroposition:

•Stabilize ulnar border of the hand and forearm being tested. *(Use a lumbrical grip with the ipsilateral hand)*
•Guide the thumb through full passive retroposition.
•Apply gentle overpressure at end range. *(Be careful not to hyperextend the MPJ)*

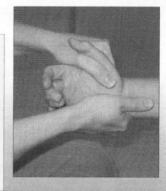

Compare with unaffected side

Picture 242: Slide42

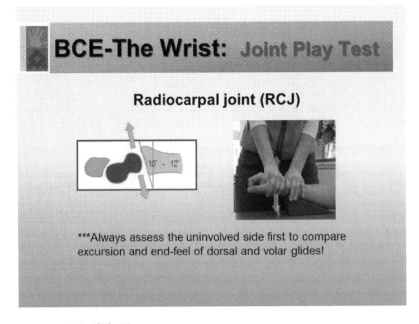

Picture 243: Slide43

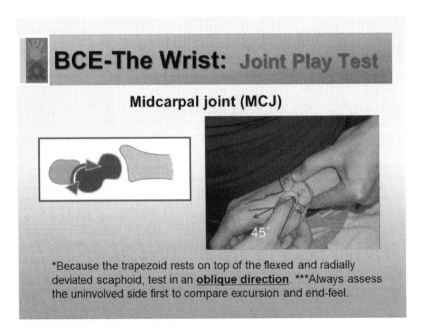

Picture 244: Slide44

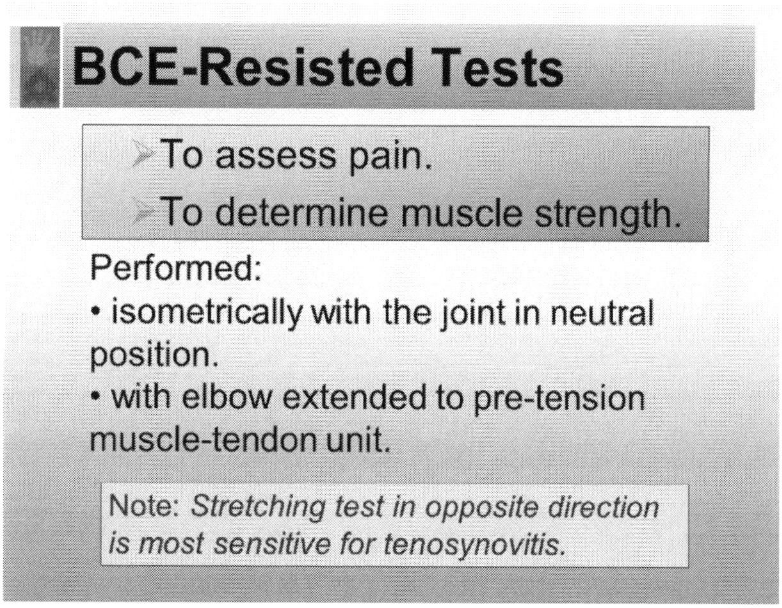

BCE-Resisted Tests

> To assess pain.
> To determine muscle strength.

Performed:
- isometrically with the joint in neutral position.
- with elbow extended to pre-tension muscle-tendon unit.

Note: *Stretching test in opposite direction is most sensitive for tenosynovitis.*

Picture 245: Slide45

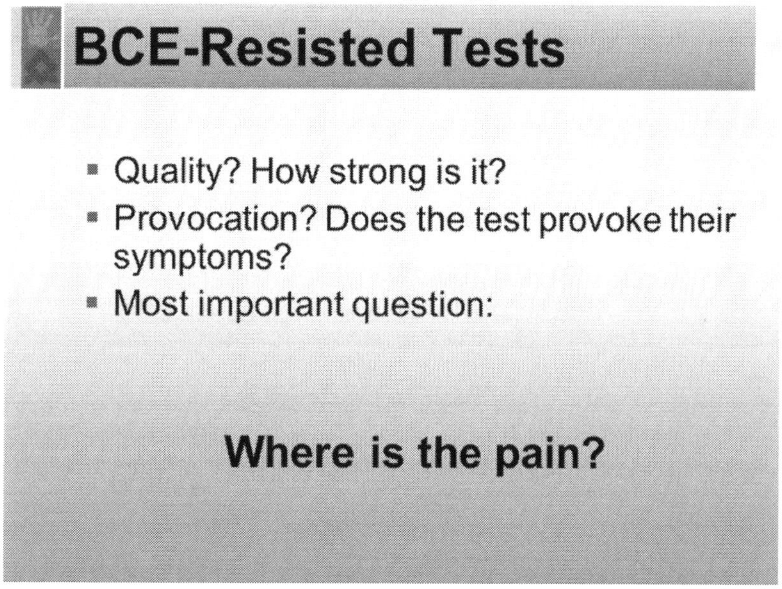

BCE-Resisted Tests

- Quality? How strong is it?
- Provocation? Does the test provoke their symptoms?
- Most important question:

Where is the pain?

Picture 246: Slide46

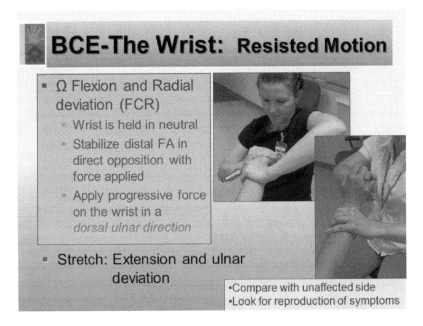

Picture 247: Slide47

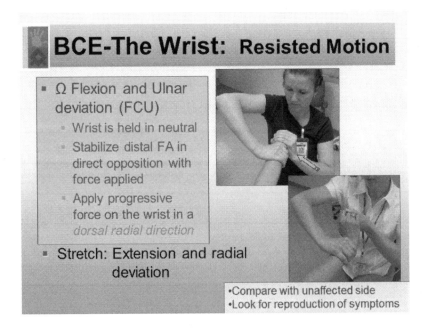

Picture 248: Slide48

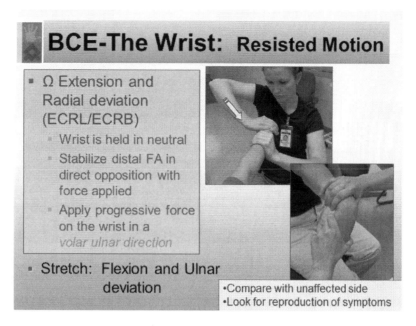

Picture 249: Slide49

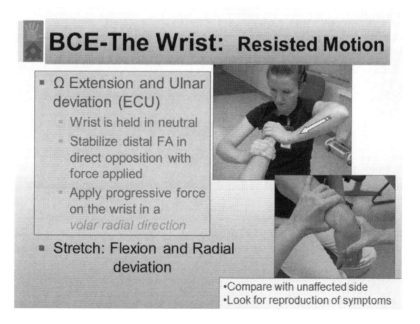

Picture 250: Slide50

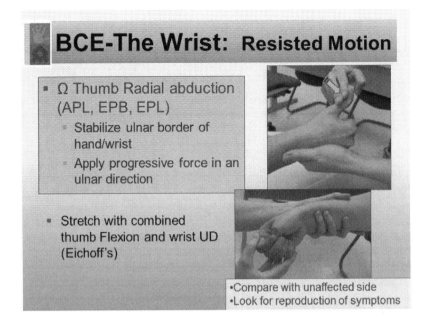

Picture 251: Slide51

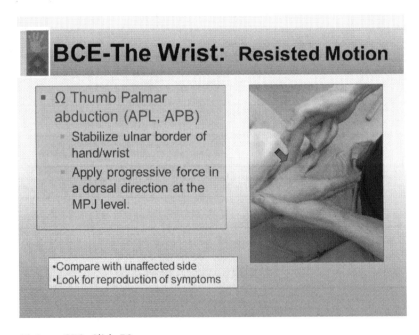

Picture 252: Slide52

BCE-The Wrist: Resisted Motion

- Ω Thumb Dorsal adduction (Intrinsic ADD, EPL)
  - Stabilize ulnar border of hand/wrist
  - Apply progressive force in a palmar direction at the MPJ level.

•Compare with unaffected side
•Look for reproduction of symptoms

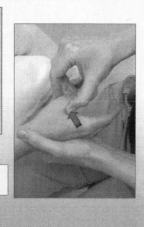

Picture 253: Slide53

BCE-The Wrist: Resisted Motion

- Ω Thumb ulnar adduction (FPL, FPB, intrinsic flexors)
  - Stabilize ulnar border of hand/wrist
  - Apply progressive force in a radial direction.

•Compare with unaffected side
•Look for reproduction of symptoms

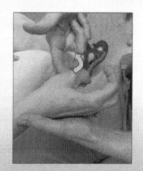

Picture 254: Slide54

BCE-The Wrist: Special tests

> To differentiate within a group of structures.

> To confirm a tentative diagnosis.

> To unravel a difficult pattern.

> To extend a negative examination.

> To make a differential Dx.

> To understand unusual signs.

Picture 255: Slide55

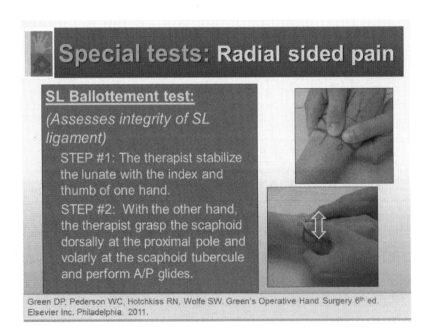

Special tests: Radial sided pain

SL Ballottement test:

(Assesses integrity of SL ligament)

STEP #1: The therapist stabilize the lunate with the index and thumb of one hand.

STEP #2: With the other hand, the therapist grasp the scaphoid dorsally at the proximal pole and volarly at the scaphoid tubercule and perform A/P glides.

Green DP, Pederson WC, Hotchkiss RN, Wolfe SW. Green's Operative Hand Surgery 6th ed. Elsevier Inc. Philadelphia. 2011.

Picture 256: Slide56

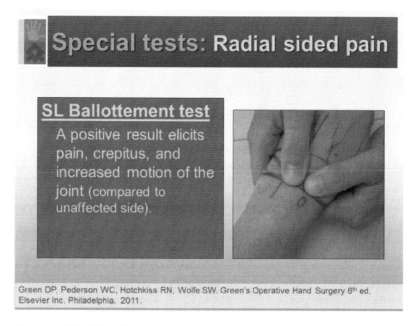

Picture 257: Slide57

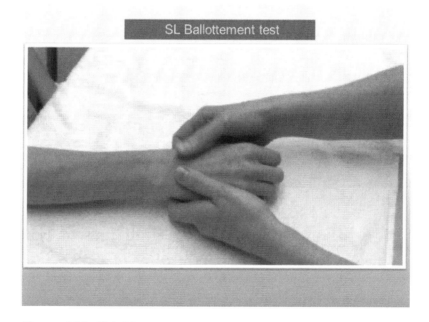

Picture 258: Slide58

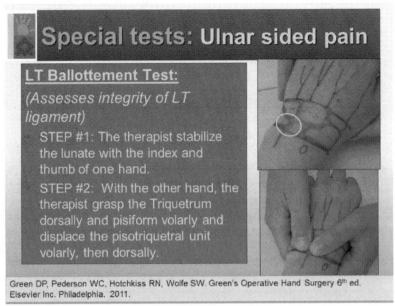

Picture 259: Slide59

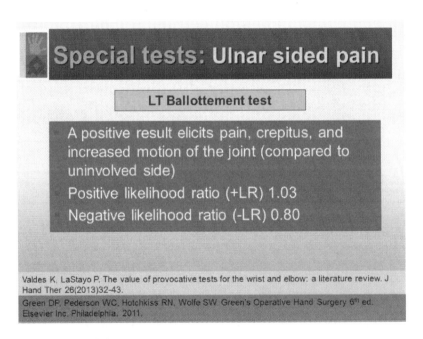

Picture 260: Slide60

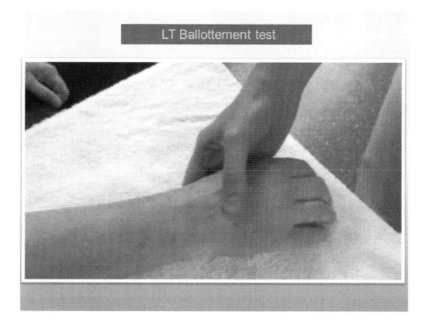

Picture 261: Slide61

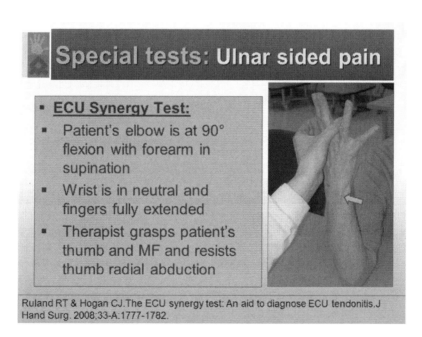

Picture 262: Slide62

Special tests: Ulnar sided pain

ECU Synergy Test:

► Look for:

    ► Prominence of ECU tendon

    ► Provocation of pain along dorsal-ulnar wrist

► Positive likelihood ratio (+LR) 2.9

Valdes K, LaStayo P. The value of provocative tests for the wrist and elbow: a literature review. J Hand Ther 26(2013)32-43.

Ruland RT & Hogan CJ.The ECU synergy test: An aid to diagnose ECU tendonitis.J Hand Surg. 2008;33-A:1777-1782.

Picture 263: Slide63

Special tests: Ulnar sided pain

- **Ulno-Carpal Stress Test:**
  - Place the wrist in UD
  - Provide an axial load throught the wrist
  - While maintaining wrist UD, perform passive forearm pronation & supination

Look for:
Provocation of ulnar wrist pain

Nakamura R, Horii T, Imaeda E, et al. The ulno-carpal stress test in the diagnosis of ulnar-sided wrist pain. J Hand Surg Br. 1997; 22: 719-723.

Picture 264: Slide64

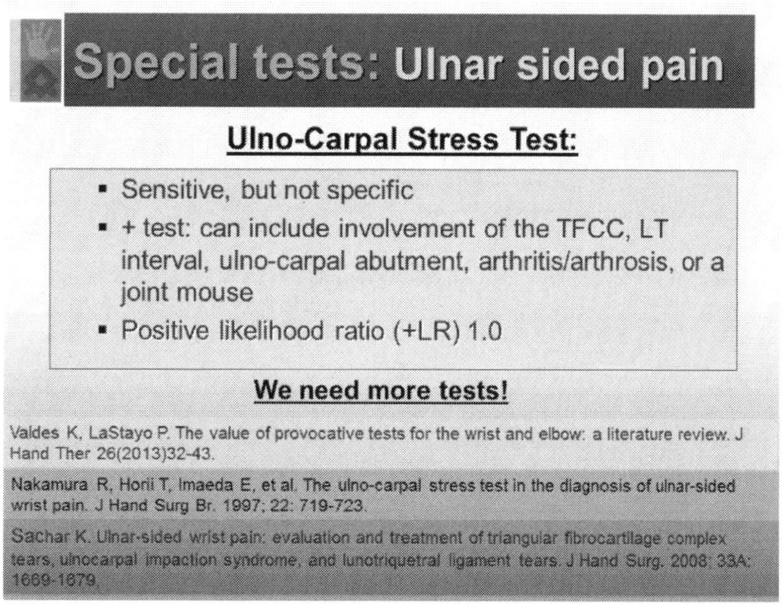

Special tests: Ulnar sided pain

Ulno-Carpal Stress Test:

- Sensitive, but not specific
- + test: can include involvement of the TFCC, LT interval, ulno-carpal abutment, arthritis/arthrosis, or a joint mouse
- Positive likelihood ratio (+LR) 1.0

We need more tests!

Valdes K, LaStayo P. The value of provocative tests for the wrist and elbow: a literature review. J Hand Ther 26(2013)32-43.

Nakamura R, Horii T, Imaeda E, et al. The ulno-carpal stress test in the diagnosis of ulnar-sided wrist pain. J Hand Surg Br. 1997; 22: 719-723.

Sachar K. Ulnar-sided wrist pain: evaluation and treatment of triangular fibrocartilage complex tears, ulnocarpal impaction syndrome, and lunotriquetral ligament tears. J Hand Surg. 2008; 33A: 1669-1679.

Picture 265: Slide65

Ulno-carpal stress test

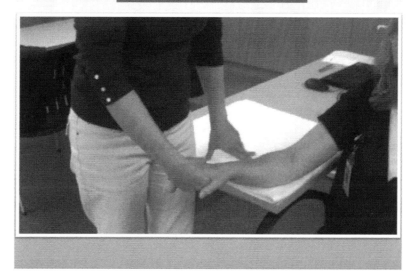

Picture 266: Slide66

Special tests: Ulnar sided pain

DRUJ Ballottement test:

(Assesses DRUJ mobility)

- For DRUJ instability or TFCC involvement
- Place the forearm in neutral
- Firmly grasp the distal radius & carpus
- Apply a volar-directed force to the distal ulna, perpendicular to the dorsum of forearm, allowing the distal ulna to return to neutral

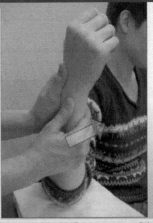

King GJW. Physical examination of the wrist. In: Gilula LA, Yin, Y (Eds) *Imaging of the wrist and hand*, Philadelphia, WB Sanders, 1996: 5-18.

Picture 267: Slide67

Special tests: Ulnar sided pain

DRUJ Ballottement test:

- Then apply a dorsal-directed force, allowing the distal ulna to passively return to neutral
- Compare the amount of excursion of the affected side to the unaffected

Look for:
- Increased translation on the affected side

King GJW. Physical examination of the wrist. In: Gilula LA, Yin, Y (Eds) *Imaging of the wrist and hand*, Philadelphia, WB Sanders, 1996: 5-18.

Kim JP, Park MJ. Assessment of distal radioulnar joint instability after distal radius fracture: comparison of computed tomography and clinical examination results. J Hand Surg. 2008; 33A: 1486-1492.

Picture 268: Slide68

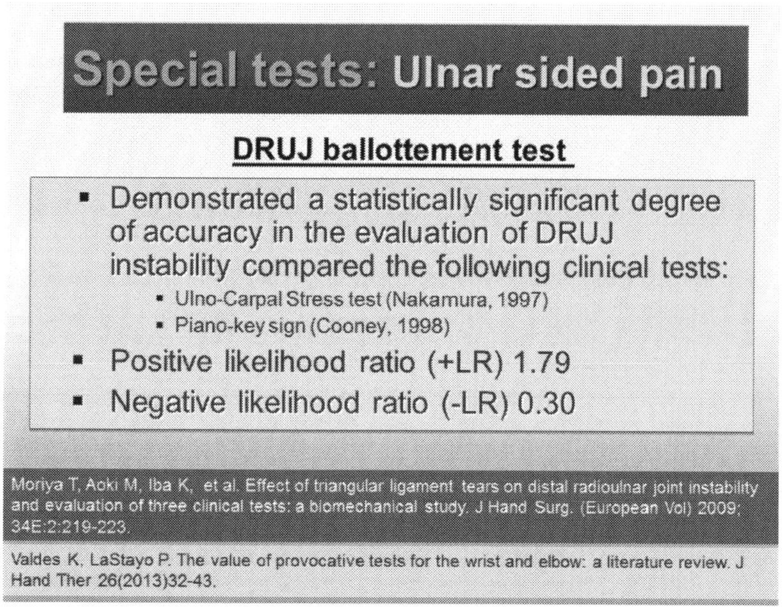

Special tests: Ulnar sided pain

DRUJ ballottement test

- Demonstrated a statistically significant degree of accuracy in the evaluation of DRUJ instability compared the following clinical tests:
  - Ulno-Carpal Stress test (Nakamura, 1997)
  - Piano-key sign (Cooney, 1998)
- Positive likelihood ratio (+LR) 1.79
- Negative likelihood ratio (-LR) 0.30

Moriya T, Aoki M, Iba K, et al. Effect of triangular ligament tears on distal radioulnar joint instability and evaluation of three clinical tests: a biomechanical study. J Hand Surg. (European Vol) 2009; 34E:2:219-223.

Valdes K. LaStayo P. The value of provocative tests for the wrist and elbow: a literature review. J Hand Ther 26(2013)32-43.

Picture 269: Slide69

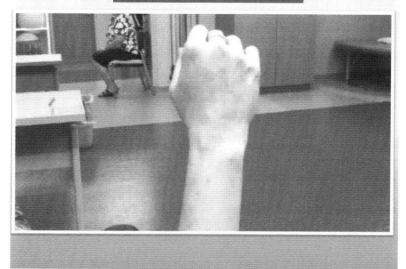

DRUJ Ballottement test

Picture 270: Slide70

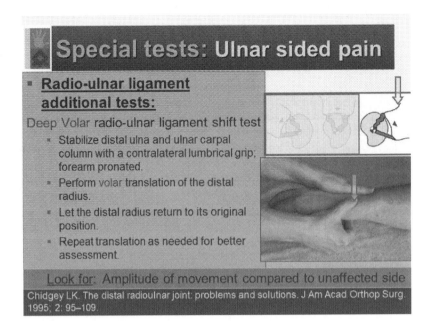

Picture 271: Slide71

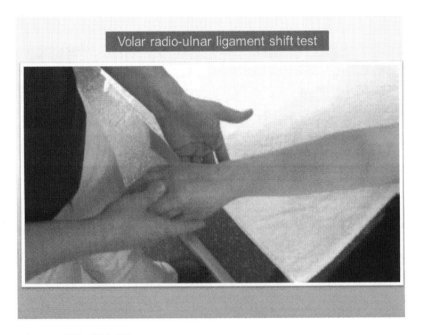

Picture 272: Slide72

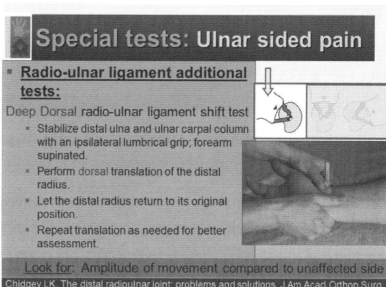

Picture 273: Slide73

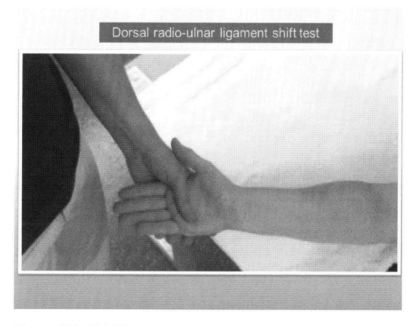

Picture 274: Slide74

BCE-The Wrist: Special tests

Palpation:

- Palpate *with intent*
- Minimal reference of pain in the wrist and hand region
- Palpation is helpful to confirm location of painful structure

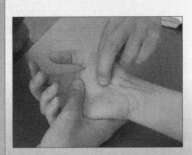

Picture 275: Slide75

Patient's name:	Date:

Subjective complaints:

INSPECTION:

ACTIVE TESTING:

Observation:

Dart thrower's motion:

PASSIVE TESTING:

P. Wrist Flexion:

P. Wrist Extension:

P. Wrist Radial Deviation:
  - in neutral
  - in slight extension
  - in slight flexion

P. Wrist Ulnar Deviation:
  - in neutral
  - in slight extension
  - in slight flexion

P. Forearm Pronation:

P. Forearm Supination:

P. Thumb Retroposition:

RESISTED TESTING/STRETCHING:

Ω Wrist Flexion & Radial Deviation (FCR)

P. Wrist Extension & Ulnar Deviation

Ω Wrist Flexion & Ulnar Deviation (FCU)

P. Wrist Extension & Radial Deviation

Ω Wrist Extension & Radial Deviation (ECRL & ECRB)

P. Wrist Flexion & Ulnar Deviation

Ω Wrist Extension & Ulnar Deviation (ECU)

P. Wrist Flexion & Radial Deviation

Ω Thumb testing
  - radial abduction
  - palmar abduction
  - dorsal adduction
  - ulnar adduction

EXTRA TESTS:

Joint play tests: RCJ, Radioscaphoid joint, MCJ

Eichhoff's Test / WHAT test

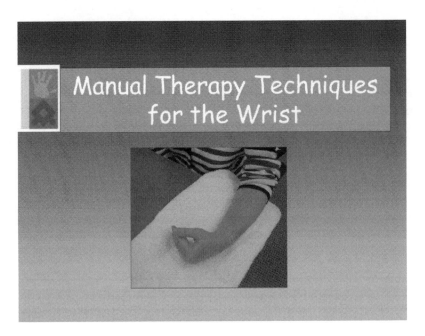

Picture 276: Slide1

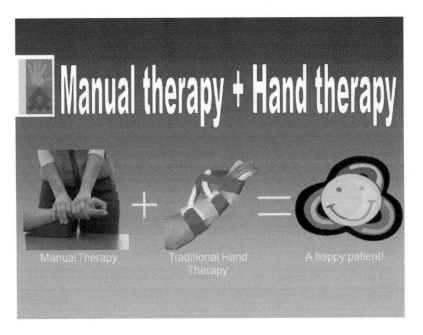

Picture 277: Slide2

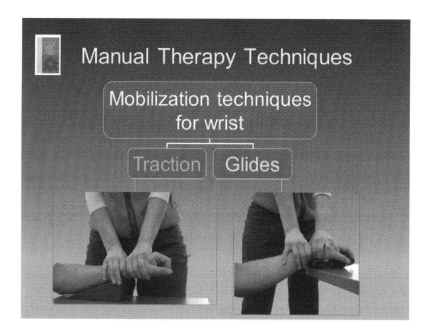

Picture 278: Slide3

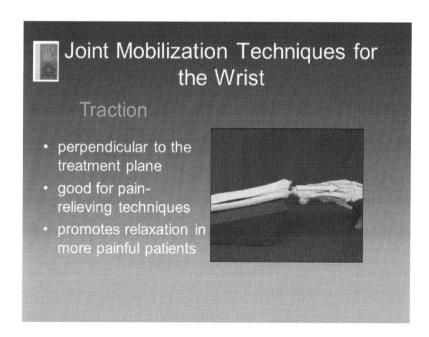

Picture 279: Slide4

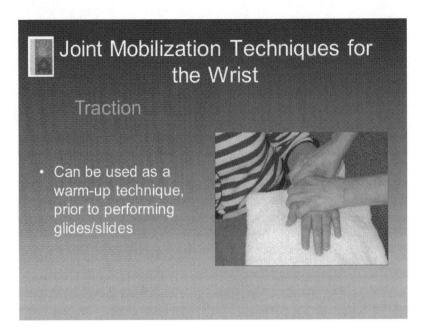

Picture 280: Slide5

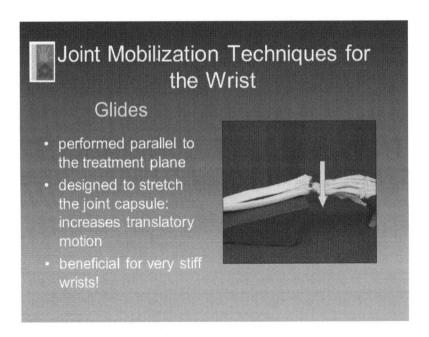

Picture 281: Slide6

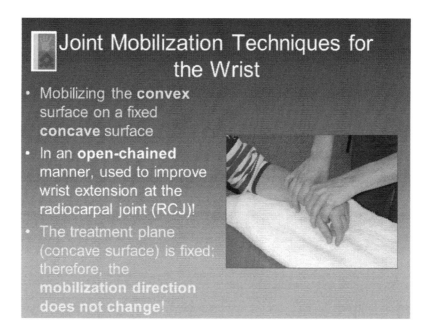

Picture 282: Slide7

Picture 283: Slide8

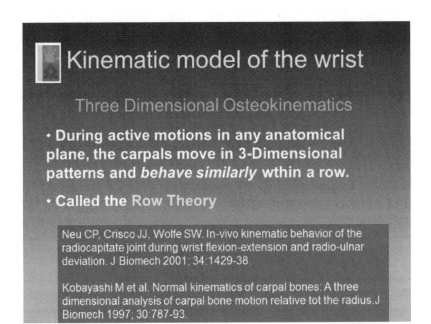

Kinematic model of the wrist

Three Dimensional Osteokinematics

• **During active motions in any anatomical plane, the carpals move in 3-Dimensional patterns and *behave similarly* wthin a row.**

• **Called the Row Theory**

Neu CP, Crisco JJ, Wolfe SW. In-vivo kinematic behavior of the radiocapitate joint during wrist flexion-extension and radio-ulnar deviation. J Biomech 2001; 34:1429-38.

Kobayashi M et al. Normal kinematics of carpal bones: A three dimensional analysis of carpal bone motion relative tot the radius.J Biomech 1997; 30:787-93.

Picture 284: Slide9

Three Dimensional Osteokinematics

	Proximal Row	Distal Row
Flexion	**Flexion** Pronation (slight) Radio-ulnar deviation (variable) (FP)	**Flexion** Radio-ulnar deviation (variable) (F)
Extension	**Extension** Supination (slight) Radio-ulnar deviation (variable) (ES)	**Extension** Radio-ulnar deviation (variable) (E)

NOTE: Lunate shows same movements as scaphoid but to a lesser degree

Foumani et al. In-vivo three-dimensional carpal bone kinematics during flexion-extension and radio-ulnar deviation of the wrist: Dynamic motion versus step-wise static wrist positions. J of biomech 42 (2009) 2664-2671.

Kaufmann R. et al. Kinematics of the midcarpal and radiocarpal joints in radioulnar deviation: An in vitro study. J Hand Surg 2005; 30A:937-942.

Picture 285: Slide10

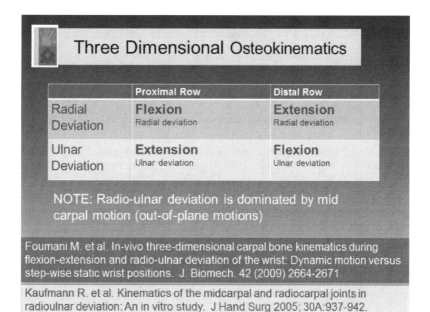

Picture 286: Slide11

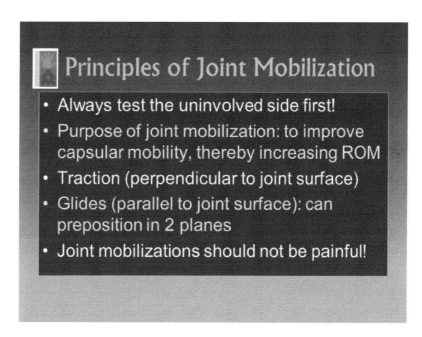

Picture 287: Slide12

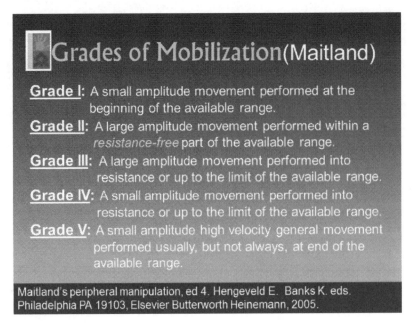

Picture 288: Slide13

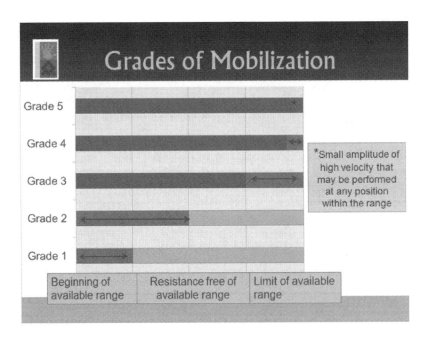

Picture 289: Slide14

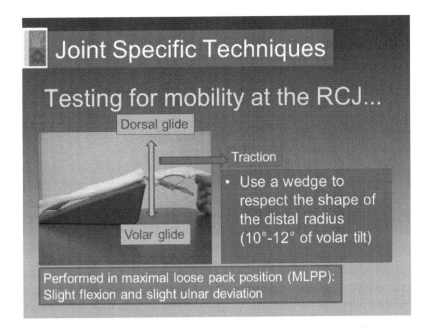

Picture 290: Slide15

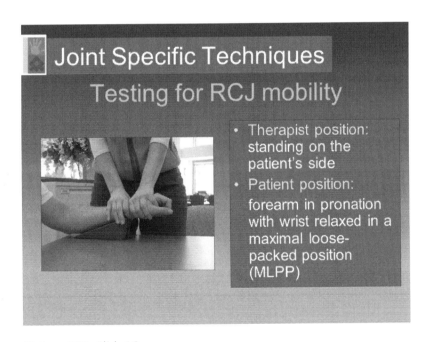

Picture 291: Slide16

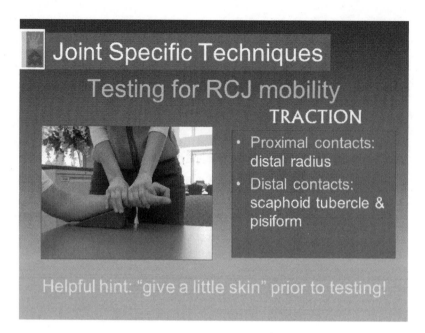

Picture 292: Slide17

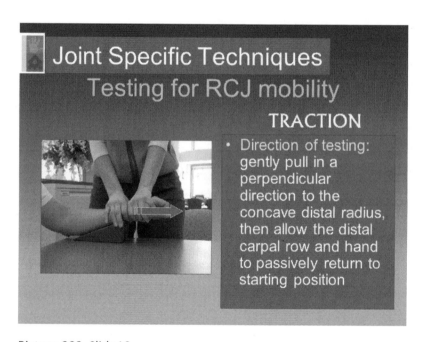

Picture 293: Slide18

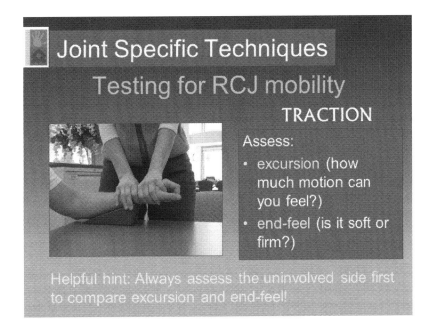

Picture 294: Slide19

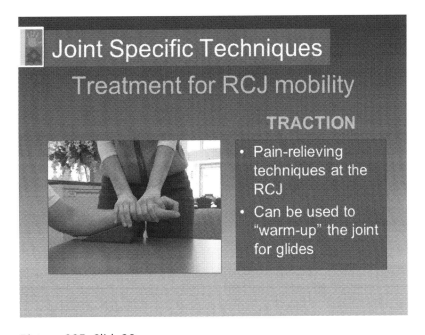

Picture 295: Slide20

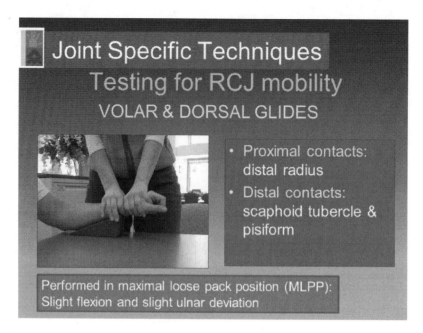

Picture 296: Slide21

Picture 297: Slide22

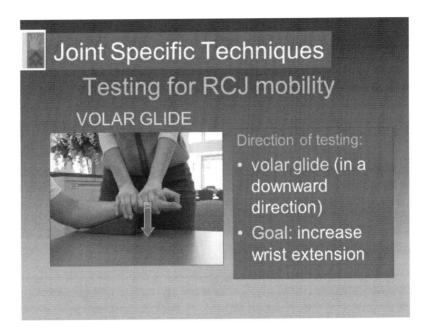

Picture 298: Slide23

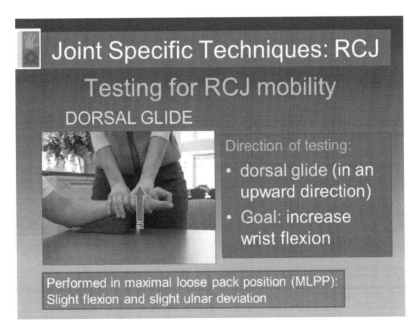

Picture 299: Slide24

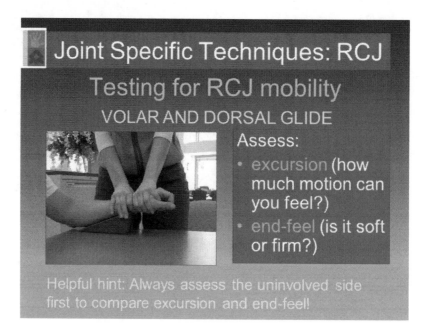

Picture 300: Slide25

Picture 301: Slide26

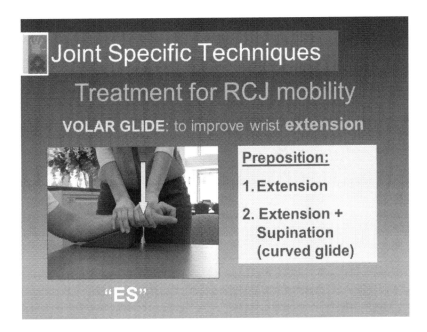

Picture 302: Slide27

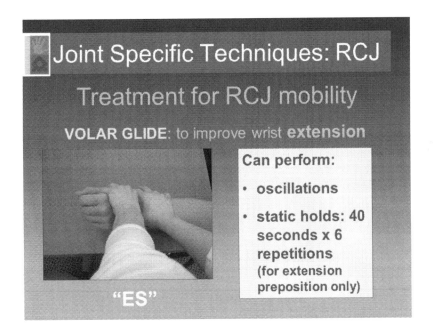

Picture 303: Slide28

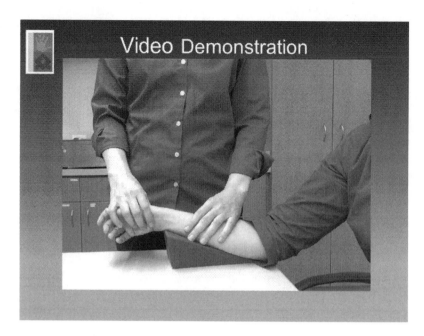

Picture 304: Slide29

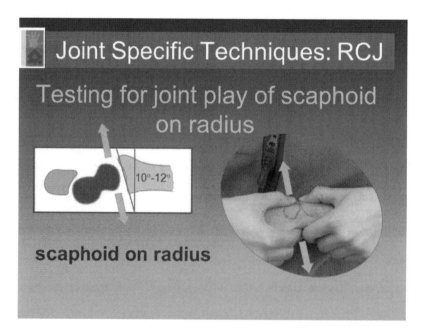

Picture 305: Slide30

Picture 306: Slide31

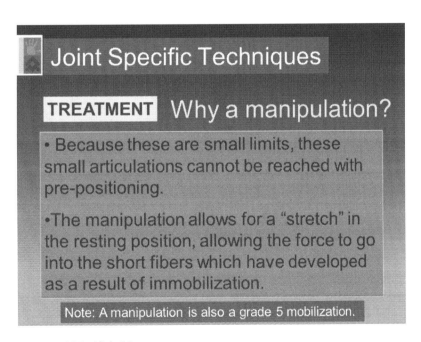

Picture 307: Slide32

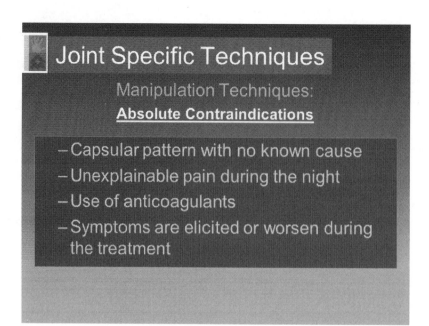

Picture 308: Slide33

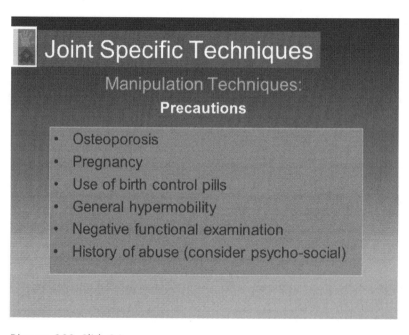

Picture 309: Slide34

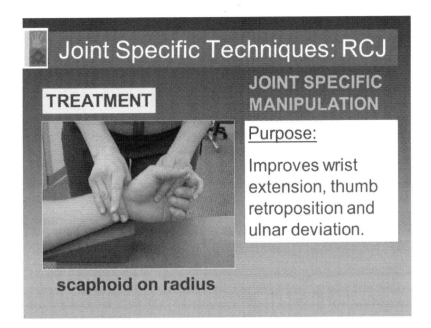

Picture 310: Slide35

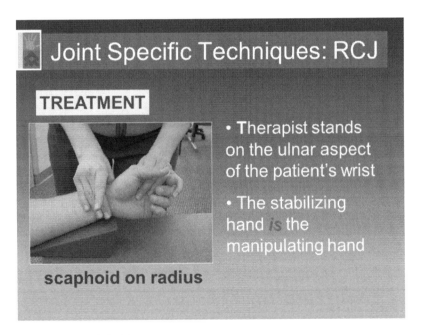

Picture 311: Slide36

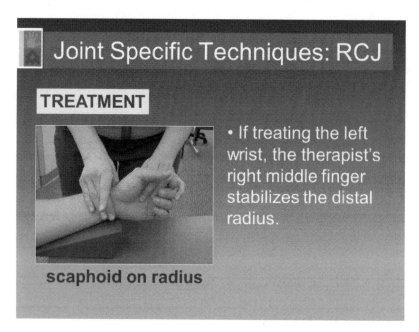

Picture 312: Slide37

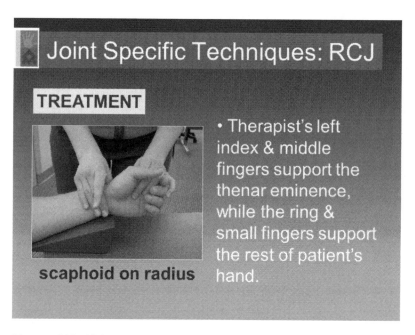

Picture 313: Slide38

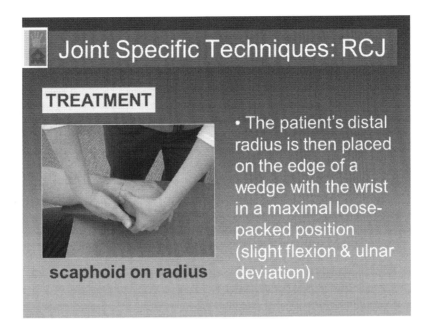

Picture 314: Slide39

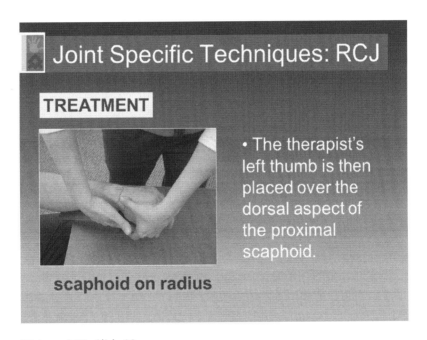

Picture 315: Slide40

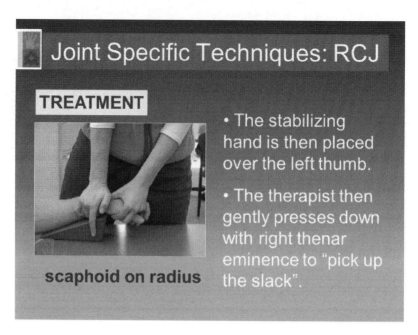

Picture 316: Slide41

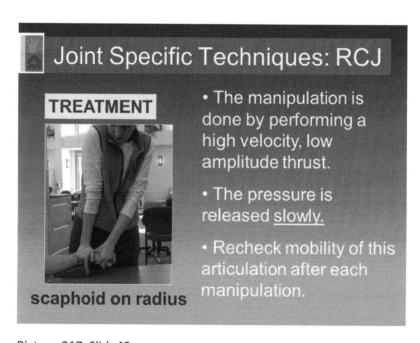

Picture 317: Slide42

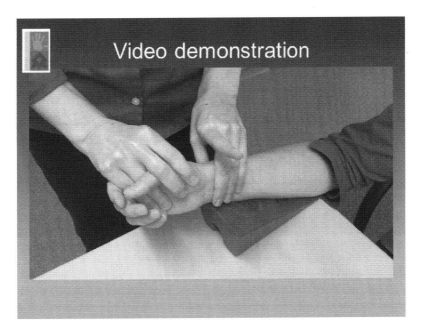

Picture 318: Slide43

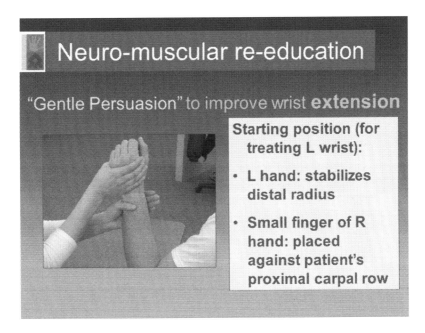

Picture 319: Slide44

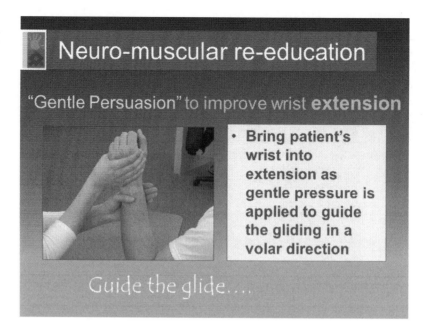

Picture 320: Slide45

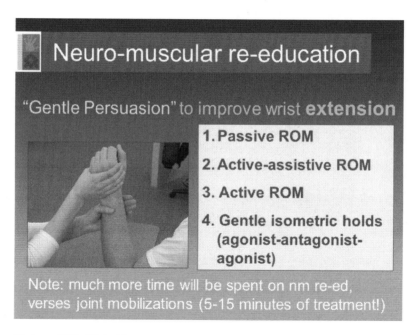

Picture 321: Slide46

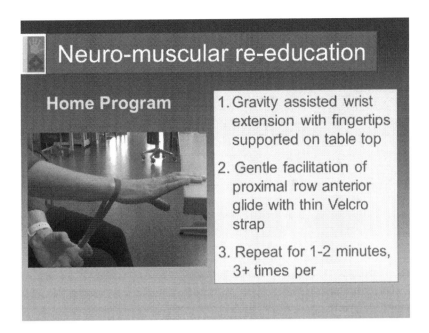

Picture 322: Slide47

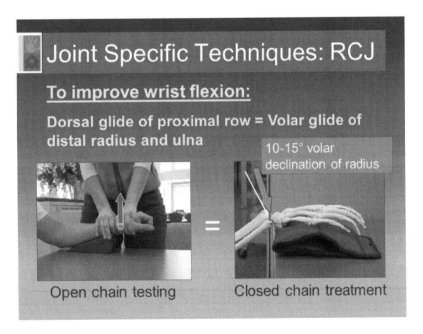

Picture 323: Slide48

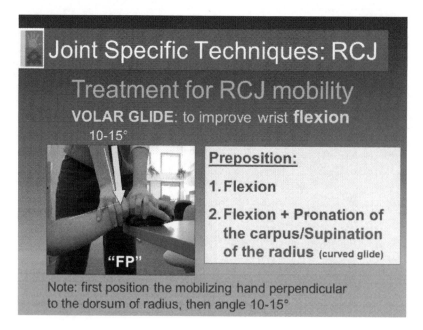

Picture 324: Slide49

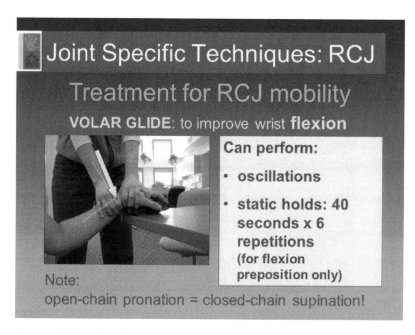

Picture 325: Slide50

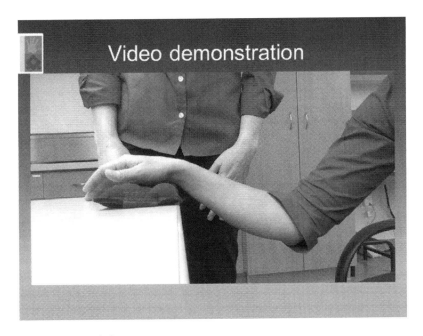

Picture 326: Slide51

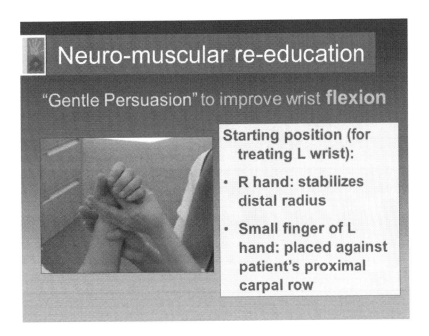

Picture 327: Slide52

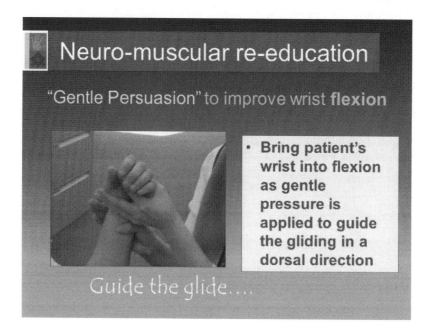

Picture 328: Slide53

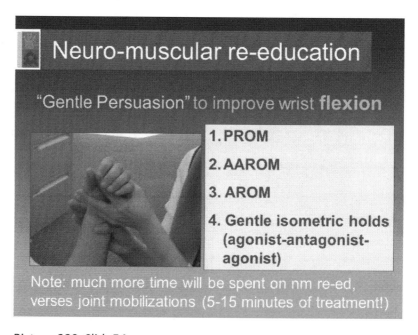

Picture 329: Slide54

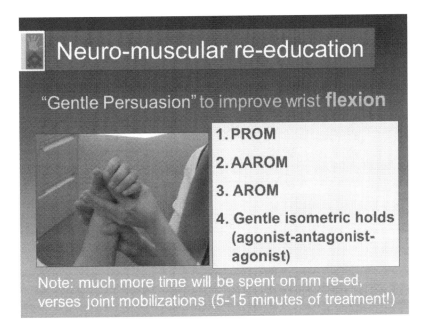

Picture 330: Slide55

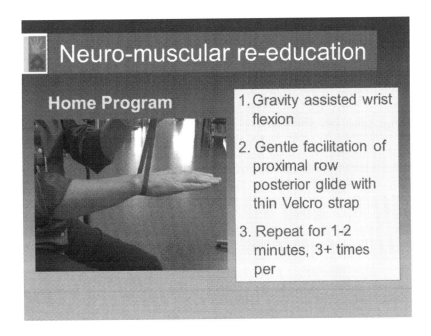

Picture 331: Slide56

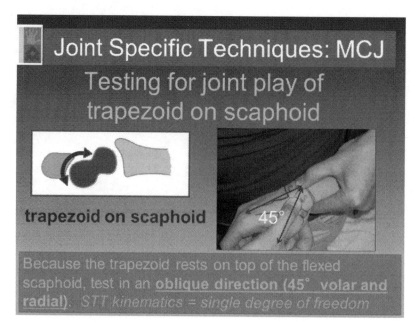

Picture 332: Slide57

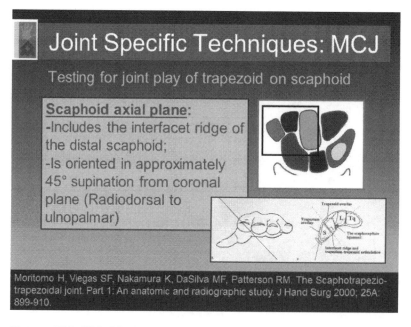

Picture 333: Slide58

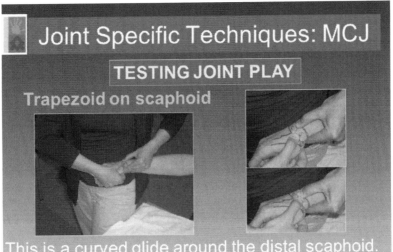

Picture 334: Slide59

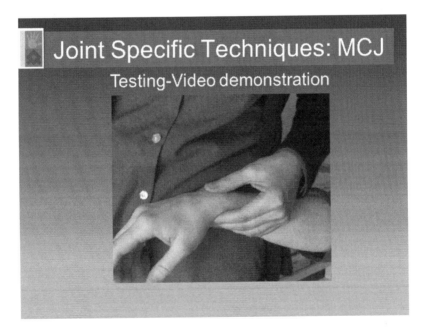

Picture 335: Slide60

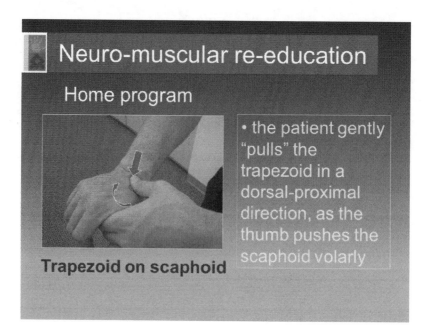

Picture 336: Slide61

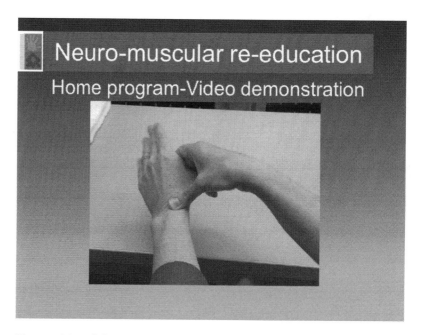

Picture 337: Slide62

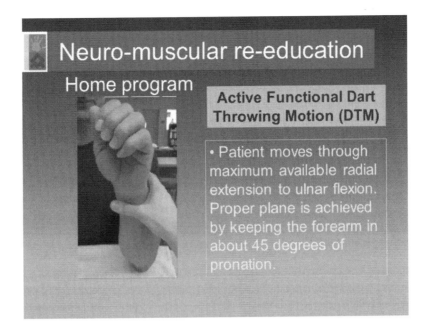

Picture 338: Slide63

Picture 339: Slide64

Picture 340: Slide65

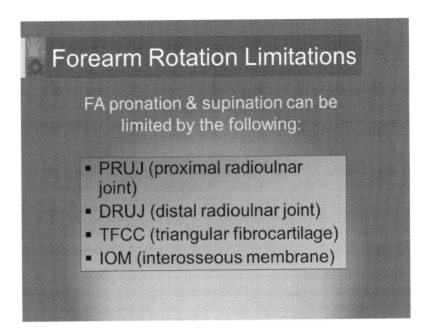

Picture 341: Slide1

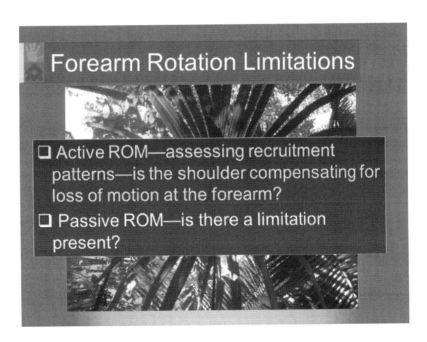

Picture 342: Slide2

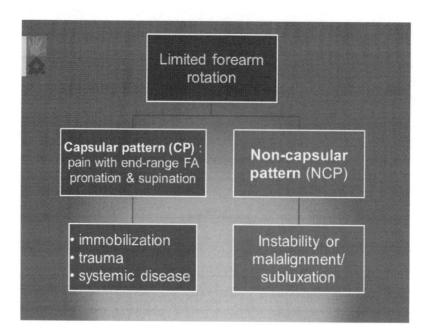

Picture 343: Slide3

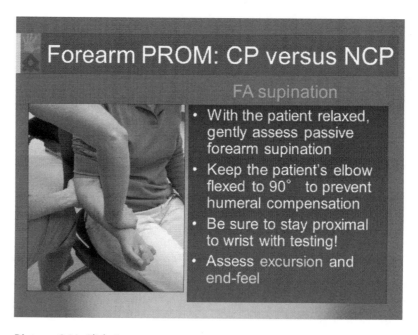

Picture 344: Slide4

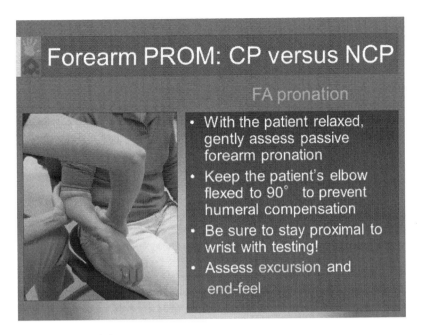

Picture 345: Slide5

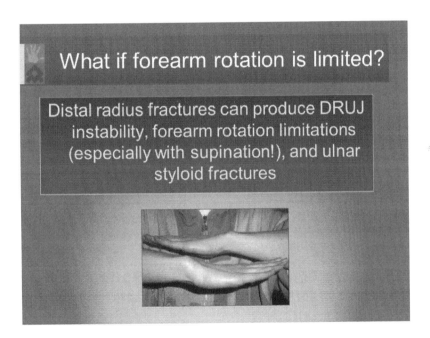

Picture 346: Slide6

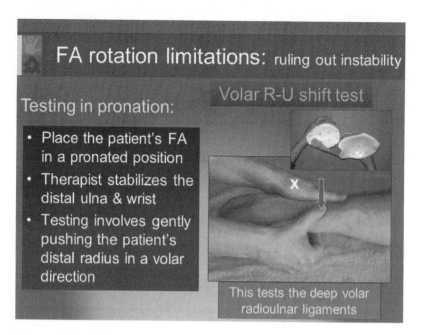

Picture 347: Slide7

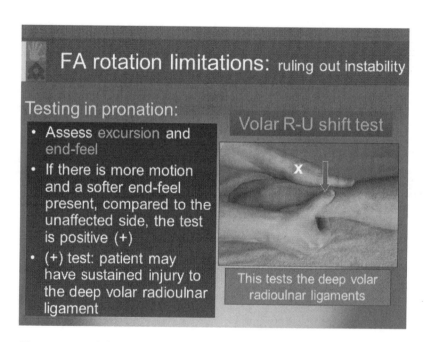

Picture 348: Slide8

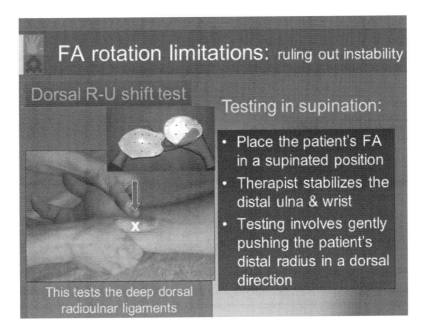

Picture 349: Slide9

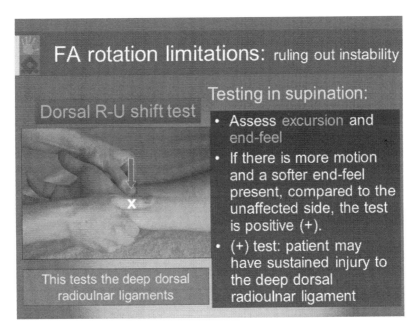

Picture 350: Slide10

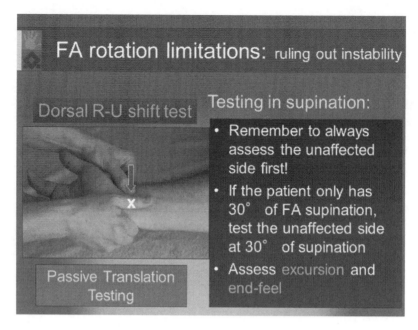

Picture 351: Slide11

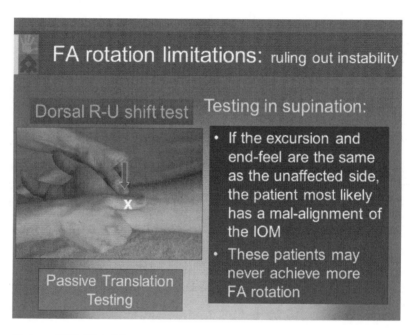

Picture 352: Slide12

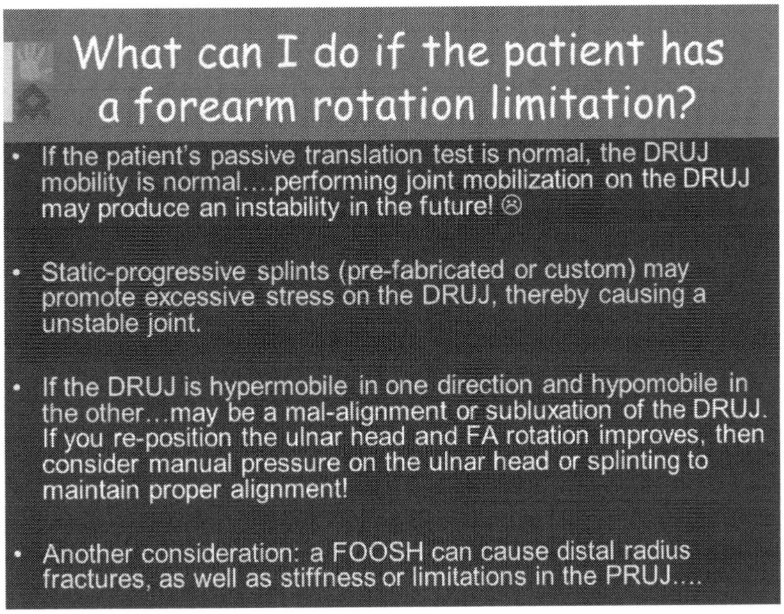

What can I do if the patient has a forearm rotation limitation?

- If the patient's passive translation test is normal, the DRUJ mobility is normal....performing joint mobilization on the DRUJ may produce an instability in the future! ☹

- Static-progressive splints (pre-fabricated or custom) may promote excessive stress on the DRUJ, thereby causing a unstable joint.

- If the DRUJ is hypermobile in one direction and hypomobile in the other...may be a mal-alignment or subluxation of the DRUJ. If you re-position the ulnar head and FA rotation improves, then consider manual pressure on the ulnar head or splinting to maintain proper alignment!

- Another consideration: a FOOSH can cause distal radius fractures, as well as stiffness or limitations in the PRUJ....

Picture 353: Slide13

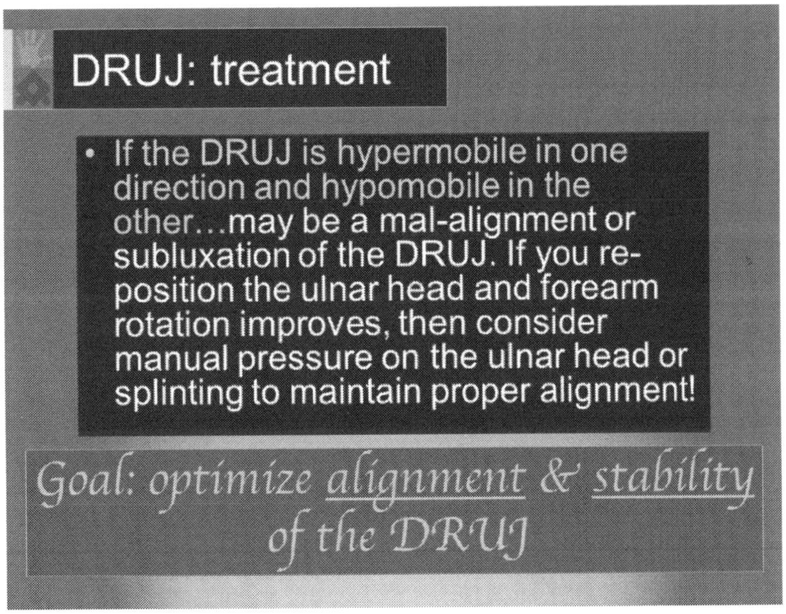

DRUJ: treatment

- If the DRUJ is hypermobile in one direction and hypomobile in the other...may be a mal-alignment or subluxation of the DRUJ. If you re-position the ulnar head and forearm rotation improves, then consider manual pressure on the ulnar head or splinting to maintain proper alignment!

Goal: optimize alignment & stability of the DRUJ

Picture 354: Slide14

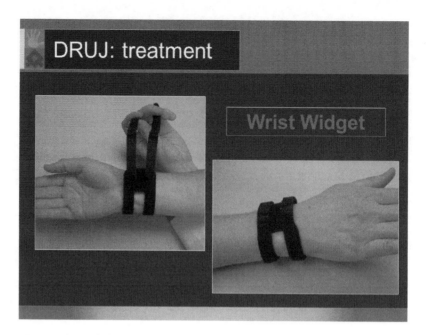

Picture 355: Slide15

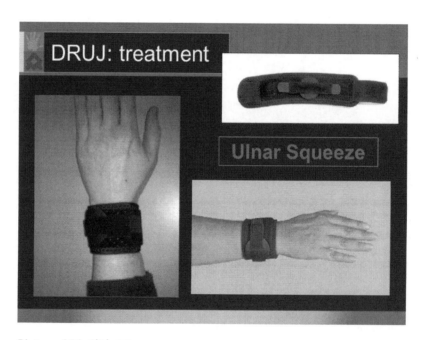

Picture 356: Slide16

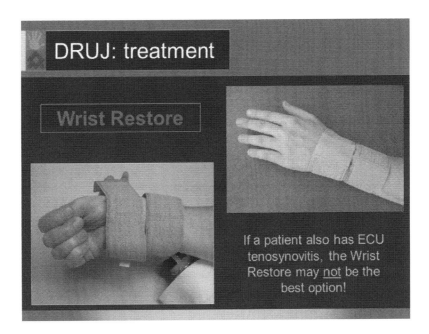

Picture 357: Slide17

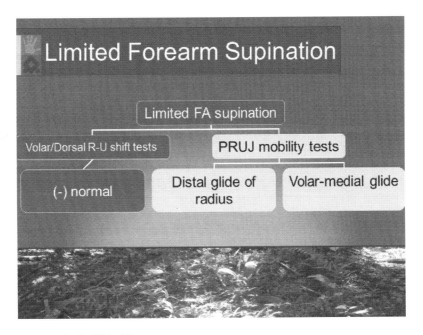

Picture 358: Slide18

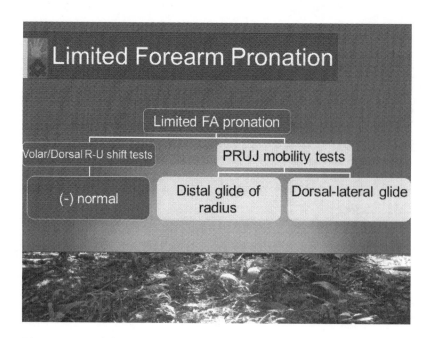

Picture 359: Slide19

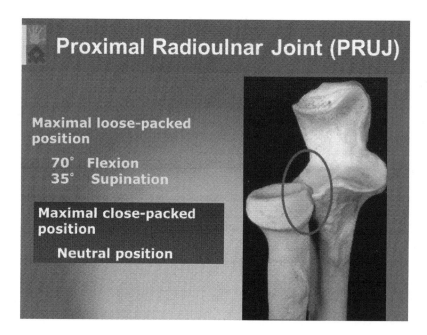

Picture 360: Slide20

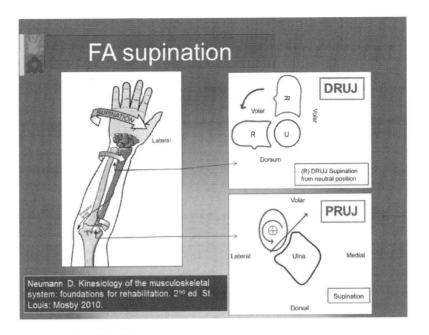

Picture 361: Slide21

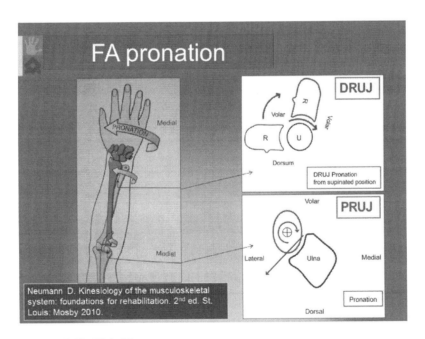

Picture 362: Slide22

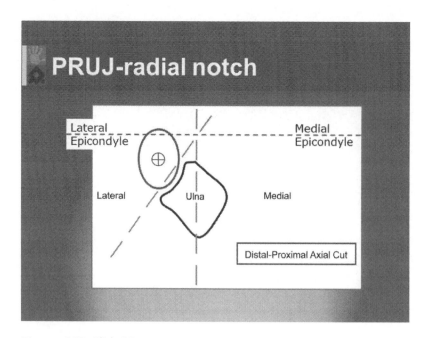

Picture 363: Slide23

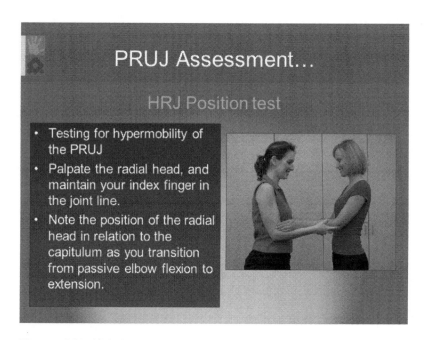

Picture 364: Slide24

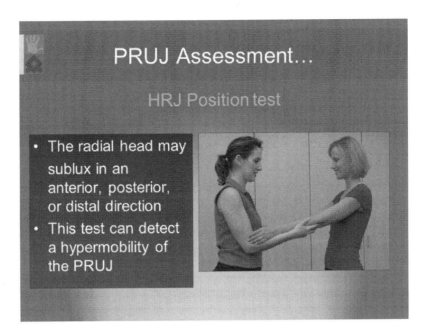

Picture 365: Slide25

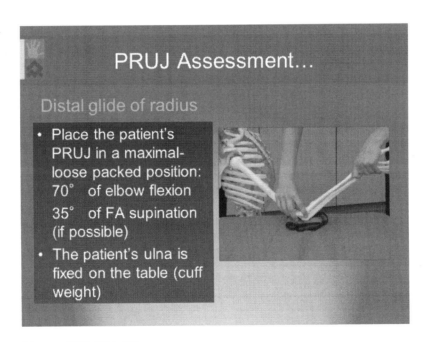

Picture 366: Slide26

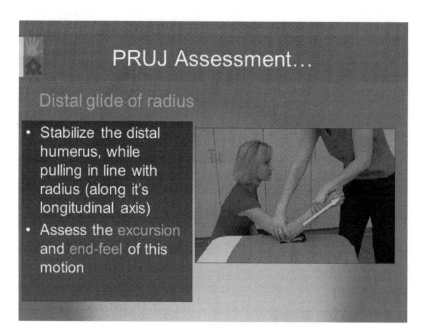

Picture 367: Slide27

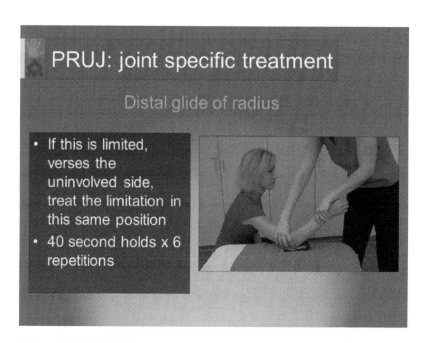

Picture 368: Slide28

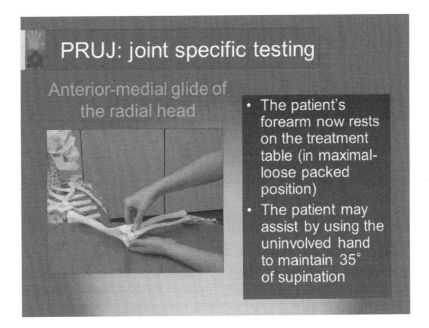

Picture 369: Slide29

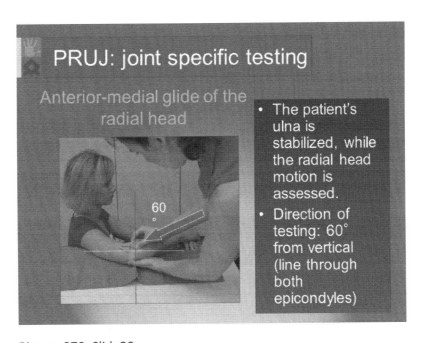

Picture 370: Slide30

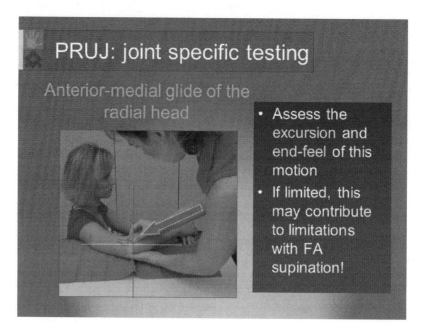

Picture 371: Slide31

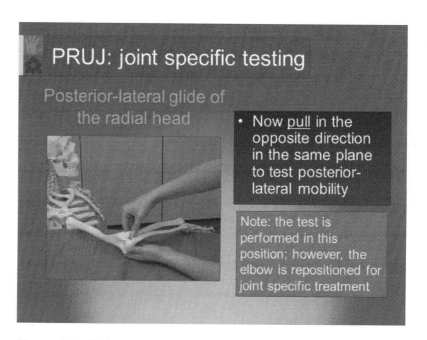

Picture 372: Slide32

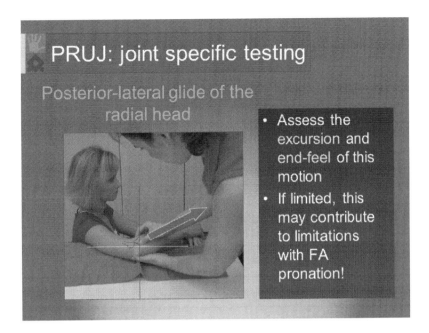

Picture 373: Slide33

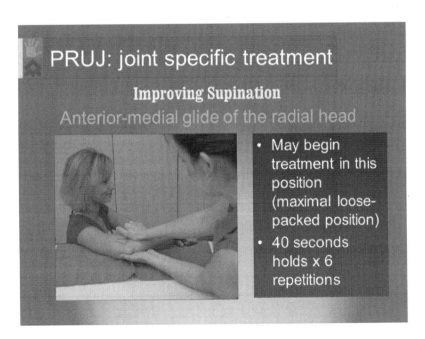

Picture 374: Slide34

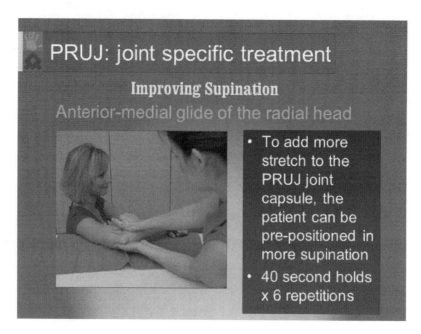

Picture 375: Slide35

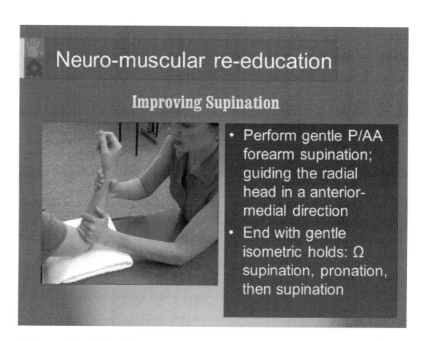

Picture 376: Slide36

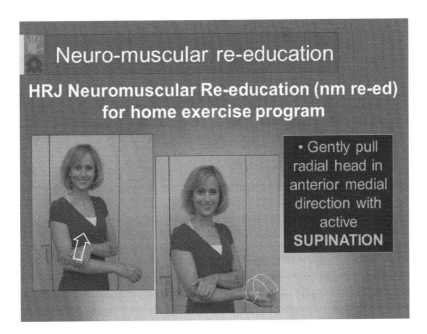

Picture 377: Slide37

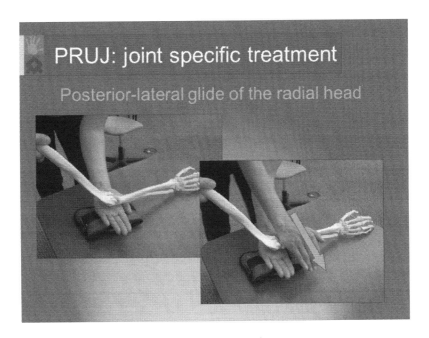

Picture 378: Slide38

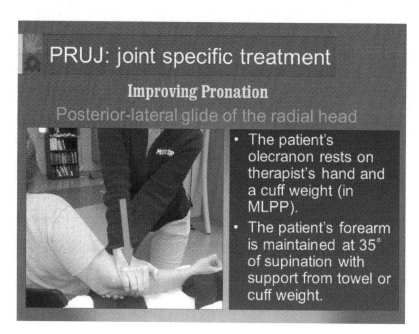

Picture 379: Slide39

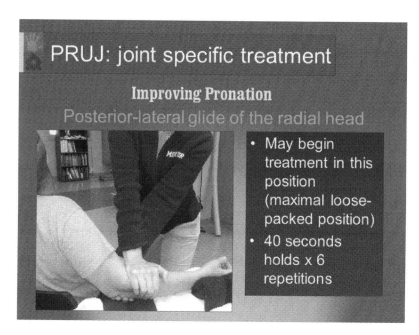

Picture 380: Slide40

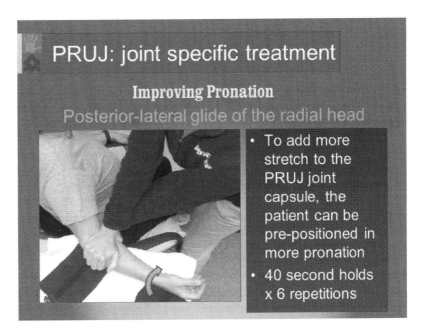

Picture 381: Slide41

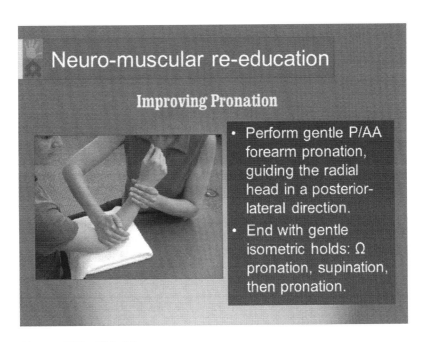

Picture 382: Slide42

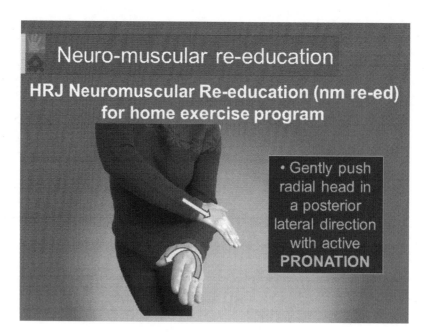

Picture 383: Slide43

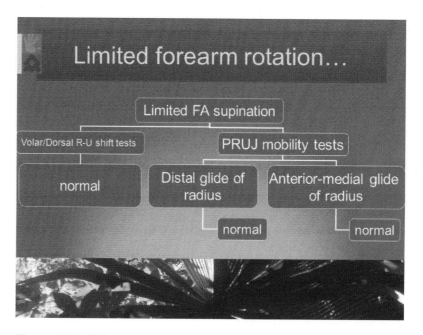

Picture 384: Slide44

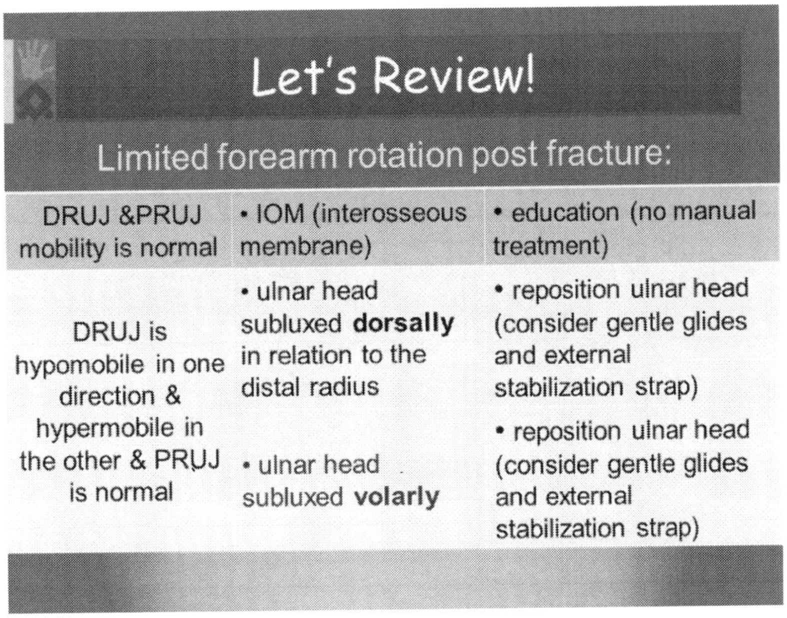

Let's Review!

Limited forearm rotation post fracture:

DRUJ &PRUJ mobility is normal	• IOM (interosseous membrane)	• education (no manual treatment)
DRUJ is hypomobile in one direction & hypermobile in the other & PRUJ is normal	• ulnar head subluxed **dorsally** in relation to the distal radius	• reposition ulnar head (consider gentle glides and external stabilization strap)
	• ulnar head subluxed **volarly**	• reposition ulnar head (consider gentle glides and external stabilization strap)

Picture 385: Slide45

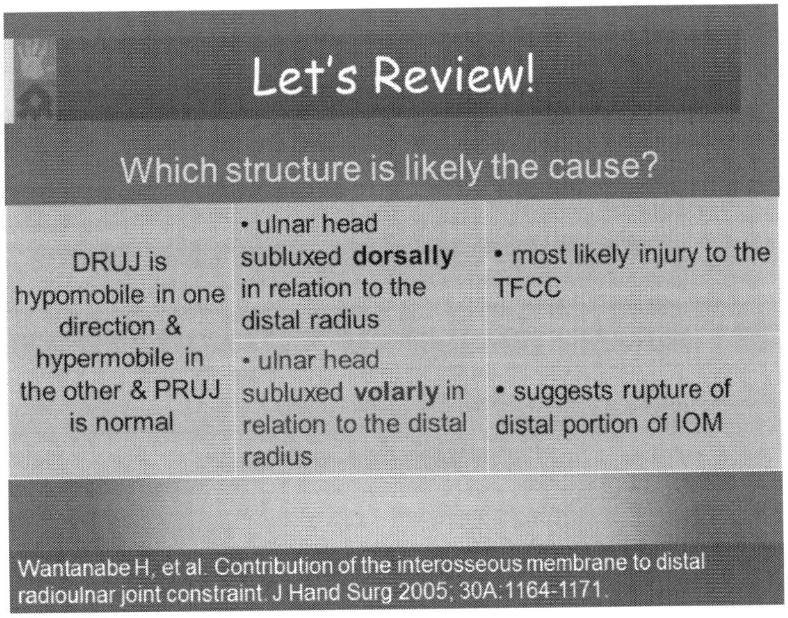

Let's Review!

Which structure is likely the cause?

DRUJ is hypomobile in one direction & hypermobile in the other & PRUJ is normal	• ulnar head subluxed **dorsally** in relation to the distal radius	• most likely injury to the TFCC
	• ulnar head subluxed **volarly** in relation to the distal radius	• suggests rupture of distal portion of IOM

Wantanabe H, et al. Contribution of the interosseous membrane to distal radioulnar joint constraint. J Hand Surg 2005; 30A:1164-1171.

Picture 386: Slide46

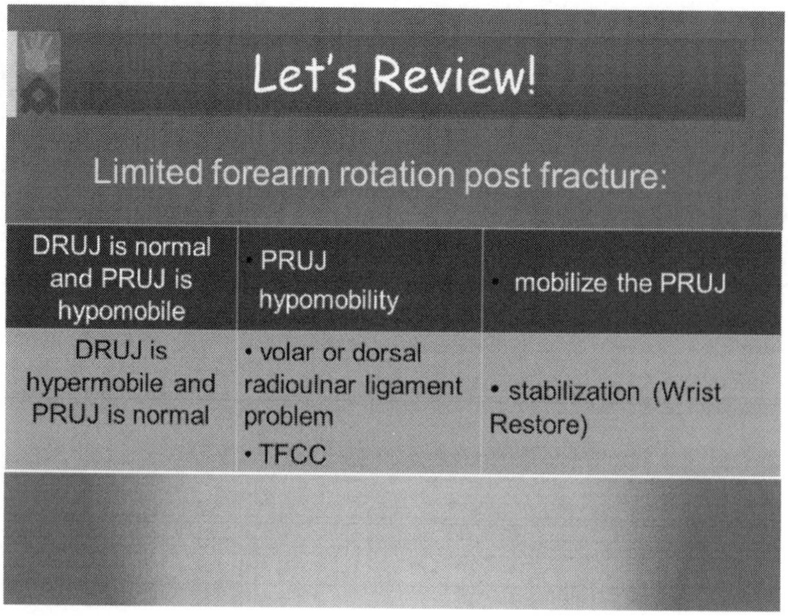

Let's Review!

Limited forearm rotation post fracture:

DRUJ is normal and PRUJ is hypomobile	• PRUJ hypomobility	• mobilize the PRUJ
DRUJ is hypermobile and PRUJ is normal	• volar or dorsal radioulnar ligament problem • TFCC	• stabilization (Wrist Restore)

Picture 387: Slide47

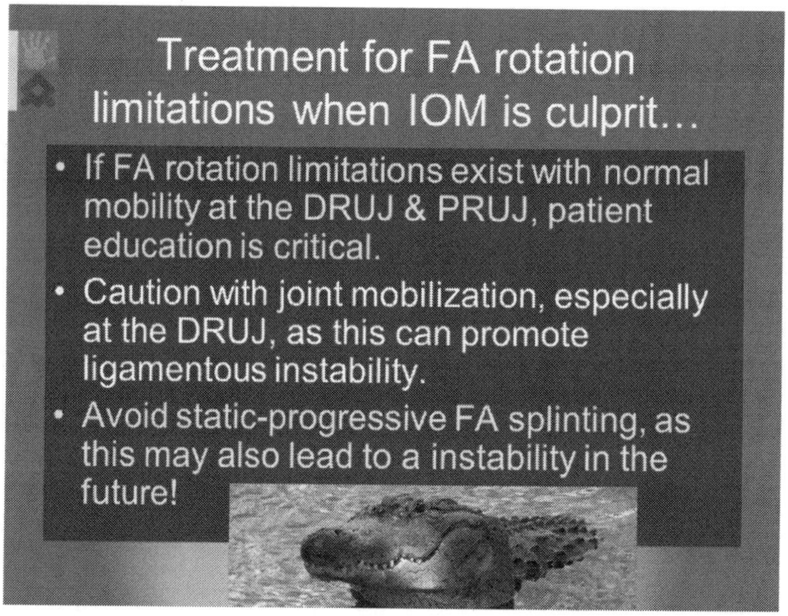

Treatment for FA rotation limitations when IOM is culprit...

- If FA rotation limitations exist with normal mobility at the DRUJ & PRUJ, patient education is critical.
- Caution with joint mobilization, especially at the DRUJ, as this can promote ligamentous instability.
- Avoid static-progressive FA splinting, as this may also lead to a instability in the future!

Picture 388: Slide48

Soft Tissue Surface Anatomy

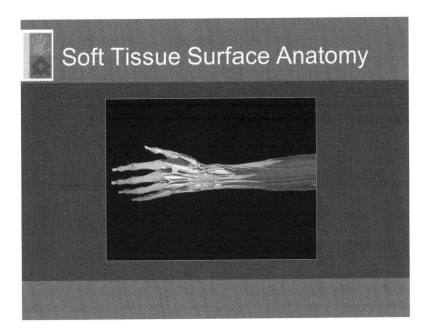

Picture 389: Slide1

Surface Anatomy: dorsal wrist

STRUCTURES TO IDENTIFY:

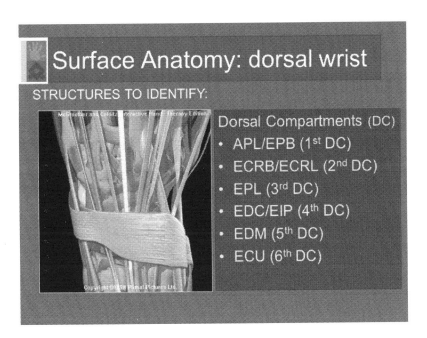

Dorsal Compartments (DC)
- APL/EPB (1st DC)
- ECRB/ECRL (2nd DC)
- EPL (3rd DC)
- EDC/EIP (4th DC)
- EDM (5th DC)
- ECU (6th DC)

Picture 390: Slide2

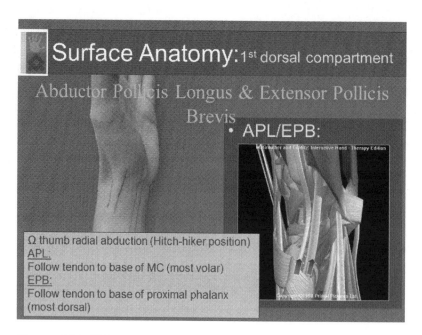

Picture 391: Slide3

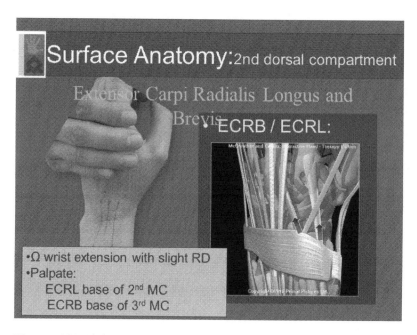

Picture 392: Slide4

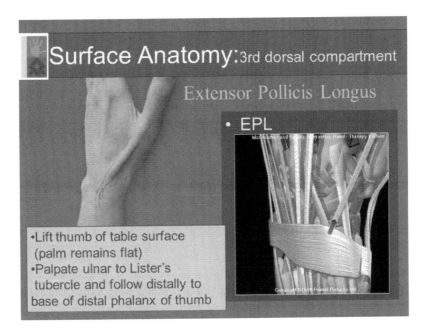

Picture 393: Slide5

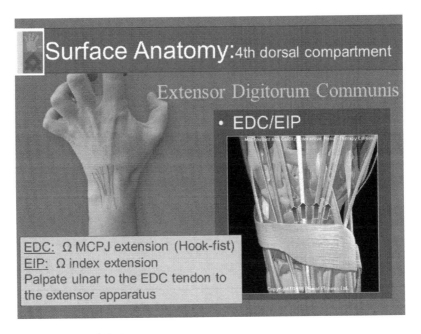

Picture 394: Slide6

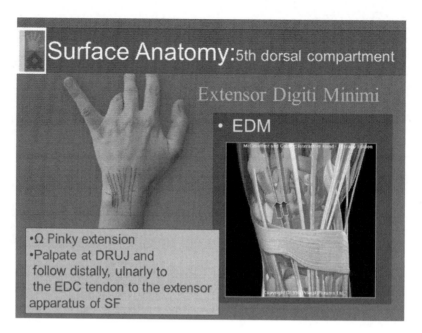

Picture 395: Slide7

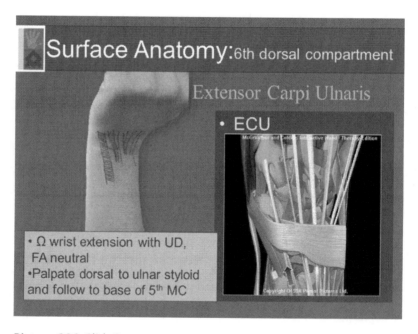

Picture 396: Slide8

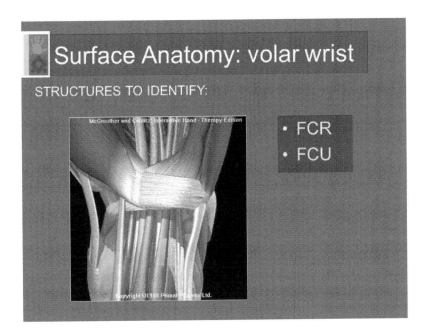

Picture 397: Slide9

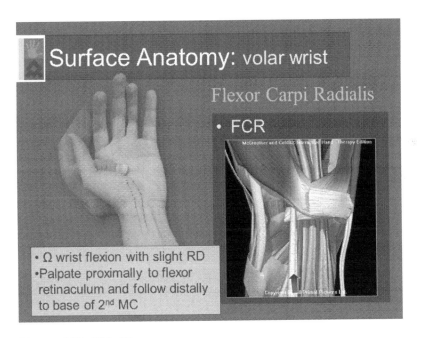

Picture 398: Slide10

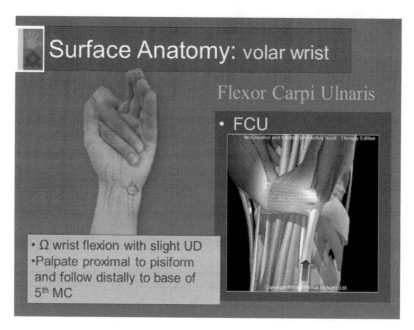

Picture 399: Slide11

Picture 400: Slide1

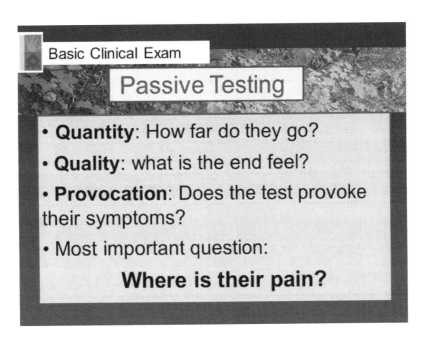

Picture 401: Slide2

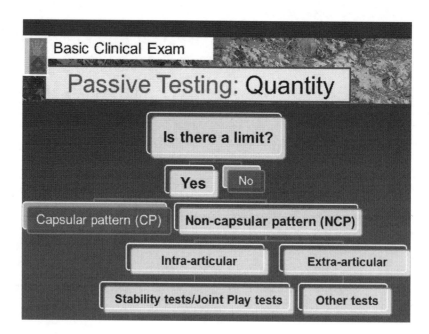

Picture 402: Slide3

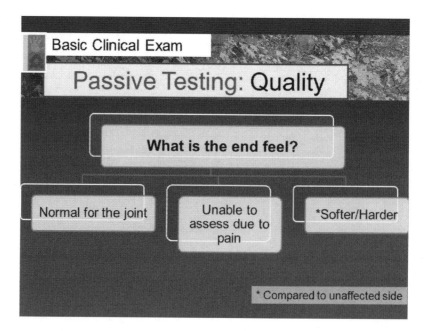

Picture 403: Slide4

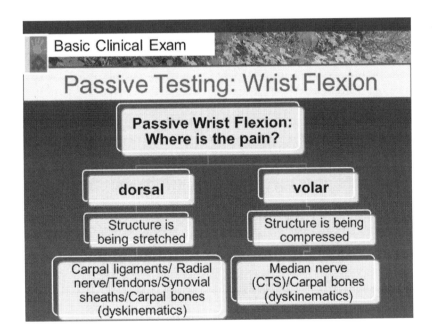

Picture 404: Slide5

Picture 405: Slide6

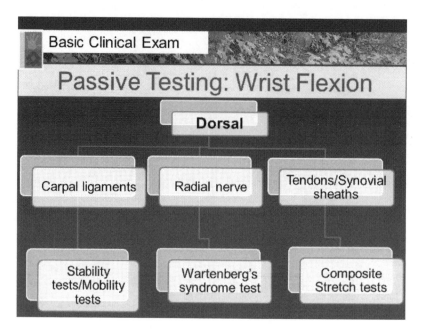

Picture 406: Slide7

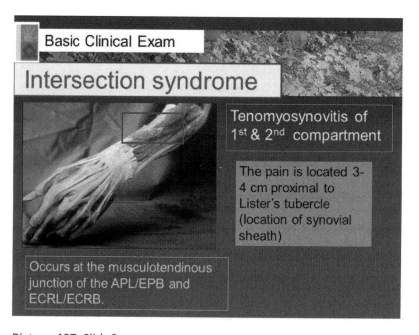

Picture 407: Slide8

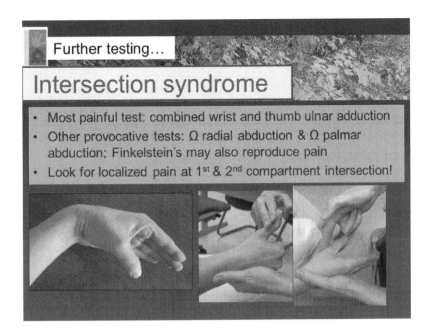

Picture 408: Slide9

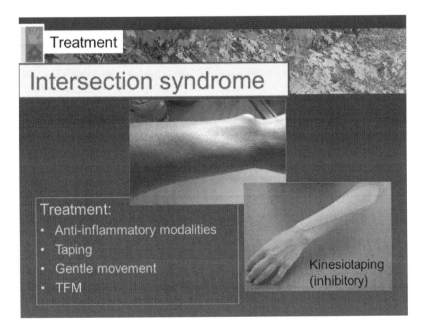

Picture 409: Slide10

Treatment

Intersection syndrome

Treatment:
• Non elastic taping

A reduction of crepitus, when force was applied in either the ulnar or radial direction, indicated a positive response, which determined the taping direction to be used.

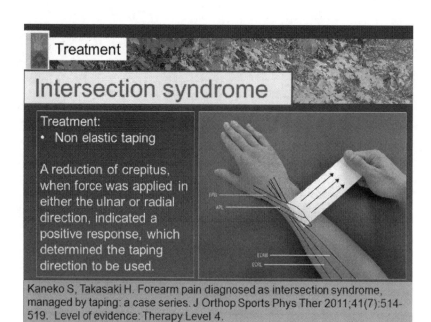

Kaneko S, Takasaki H. Forearm pain diagnosed as intersection syndrome, managed by taping: a case series. J Orthop Sports Phys Ther 2011;41(7):514-519. Level of evidence: Therapy Level 4.

Picture 410: Slide11

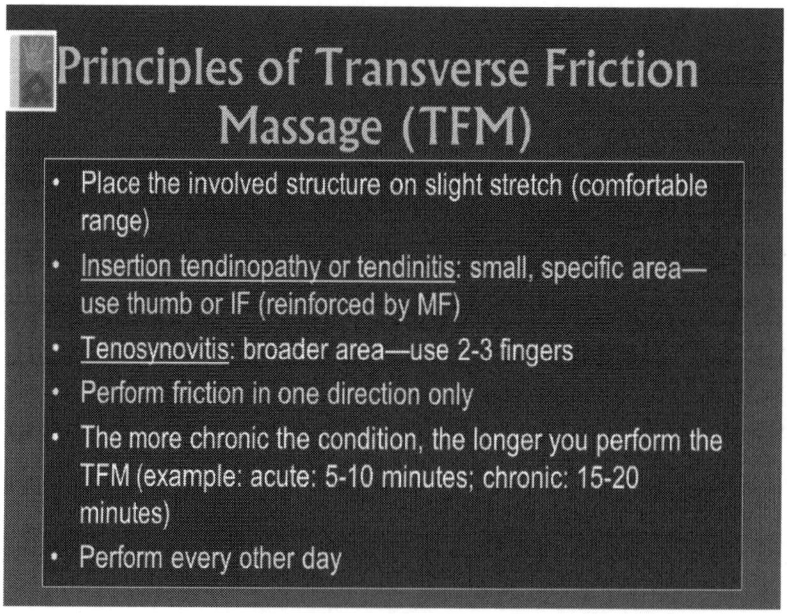

Principles of Transverse Friction Massage (TFM)

• Place the involved structure on slight stretch (comfortable range)
• <u>Insertion tendinopathy or tendinitis</u>: small, specific area—use thumb or IF (reinforced by MF)
• <u>Tenosynovitis</u>: broader area—use 2-3 fingers
• Perform friction in one direction only
• The more chronic the condition, the longer you perform the TFM (example: acute: 5-10 minutes; chronic: 15-20 minutes)
• Perform every other day

Picture 411: Slide12

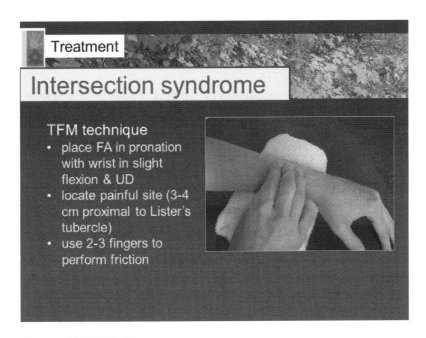

Picture 412: Slide13

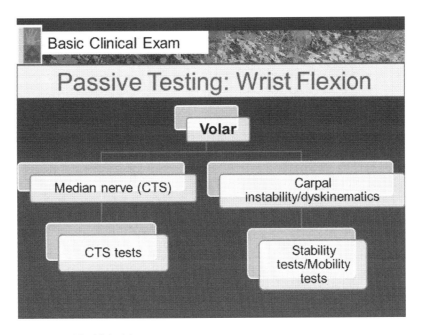

Picture 413: Slide14

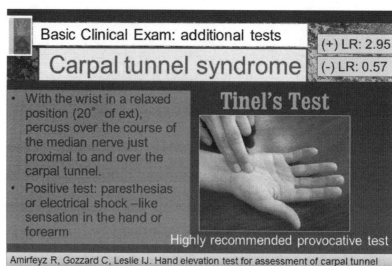

Basic Clinical Exam: additional tests

(+) LR: 2.95
(-) LR: 0.57

Carpal tunnel syndrome

Tinel's Test

- With the wrist in a relaxed position (20° of ext), percuss over the course of the median nerve just proximal to and over the carpal tunnel.
- Positive test: paresthesias or electrical shock –like sensation in the hand or forearm

Highly recommended provocative test

Amirfeyz R, Gozzard C, Leslie IJ. Hand elevation test for assessment of carpal tunnel syndrome. J Hand Surg Br. 2005; 30:361-364.

Valdes K & LaStayo P. The value of provocative tests for the wrist and elbow: a literature review. J Hand Ther. 2013; 26:32-42.

Picture 414: Slide15

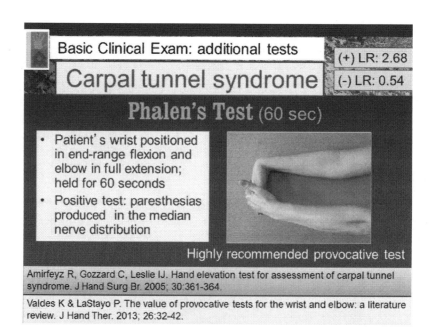

Basic Clinical Exam: additional tests

(+) LR: 2.68
(-) LR: 0.54

Carpal tunnel syndrome

Phalen's Test (60 sec)

- Patient's wrist positioned in end-range flexion and elbow in full extension; held for 60 seconds
- Positive test: paresthesias produced in the median nerve distribution

Highly recommended provocative test

Amirfeyz R, Gozzard C, Leslie IJ. Hand elevation test for assessment of carpal tunnel syndrome. J Hand Surg Br. 2005; 30:361-364.

Valdes K & LaStayo P. The value of provocative tests for the wrist and elbow: a literature review. J Hand Ther. 2013; 26:32-42.

Picture 415: Slide16

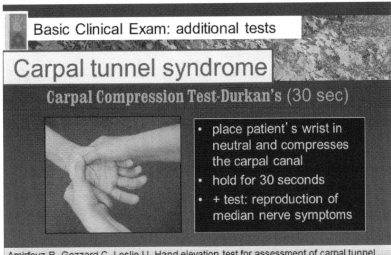

Picture 416: Slide17

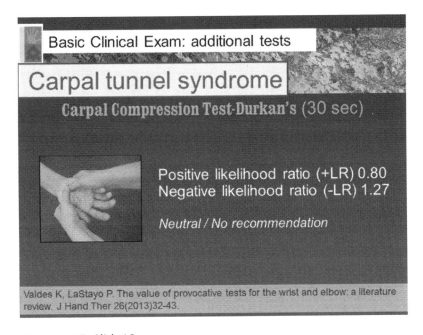

Picture 417: Slide18

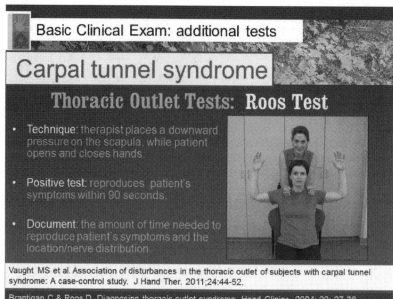

Picture 418: Slide19

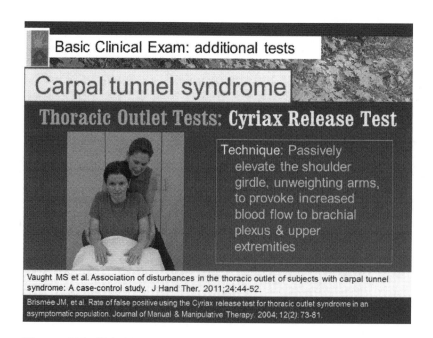

Picture 419: Slide20

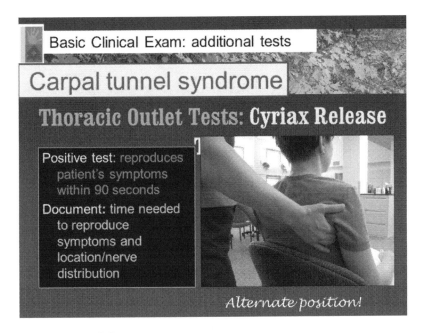

Picture 420: Slide21

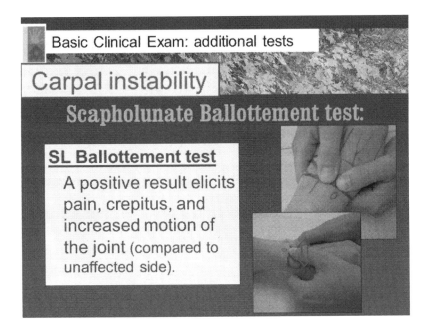

Picture 421: Slide22

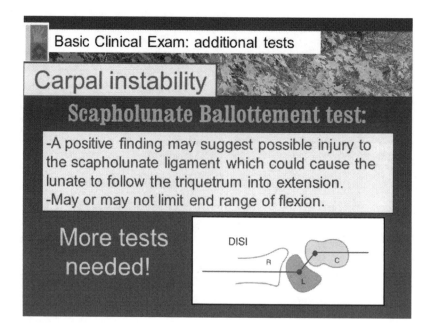

Picture 422: Slide23

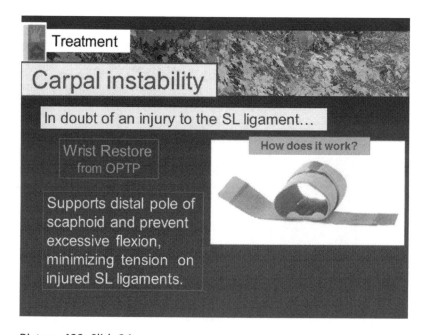

Picture 423: Slide24

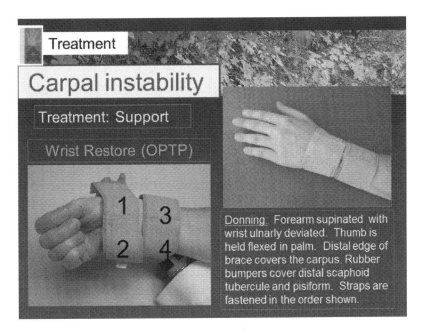

Picture 424: Slide25

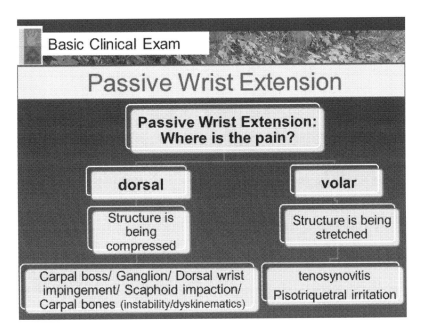

Picture 425: Slide26

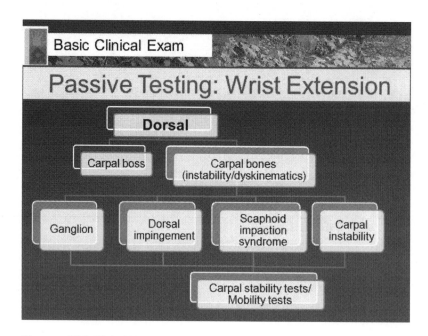

Picture 426: Slide27

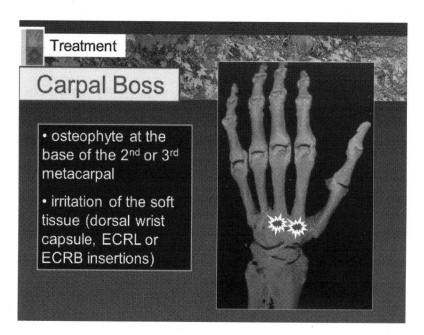

Picture 427: Slide28

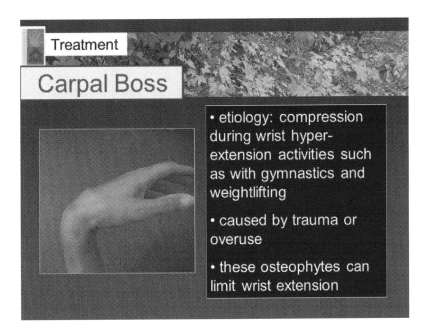

Picture 428: Slide29

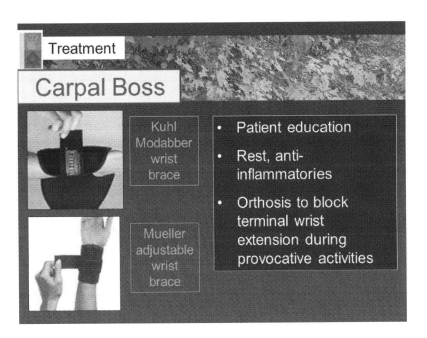

Picture 429: Slide30

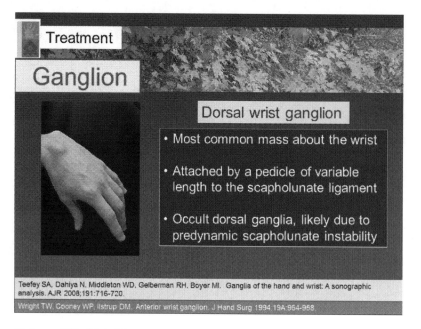

Picture 430: Slide31

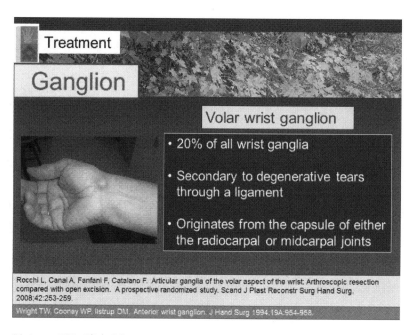

Picture 431: Slide32

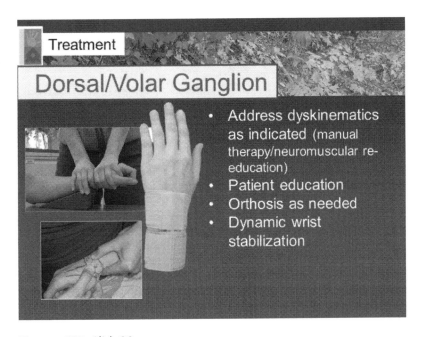

Picture 432: Slide33

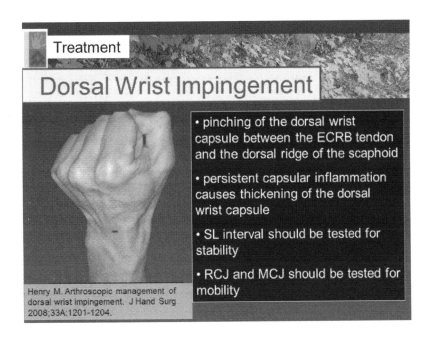

Picture 433: Slide34

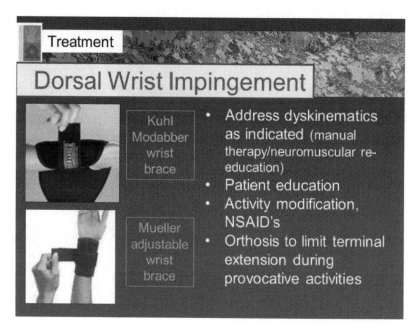

Picture 434: Slide35

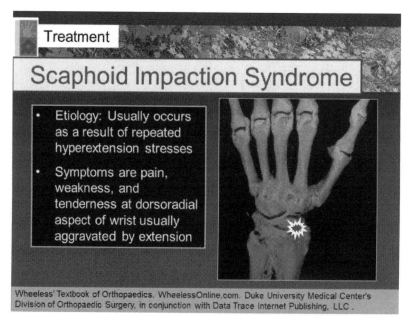

Picture 435: Slide36

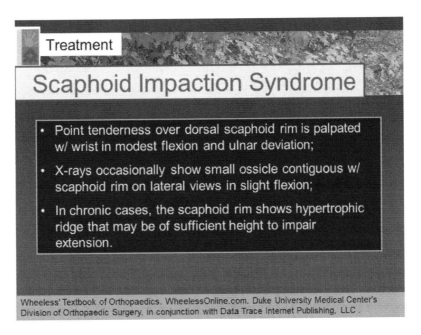

Picture 436: Slide37

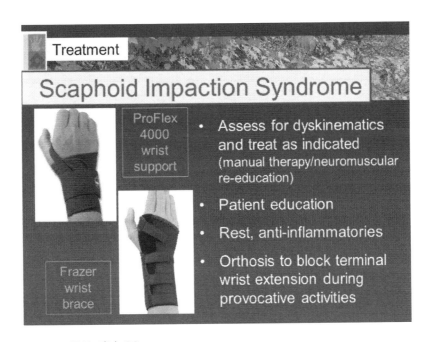

Picture 437: Slide38

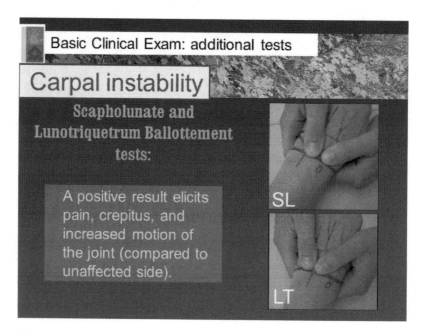

Picture 438: Slide39

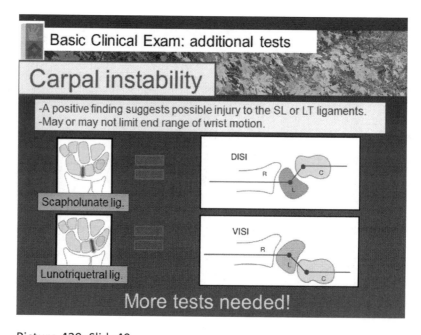

Picture 439: Slide40

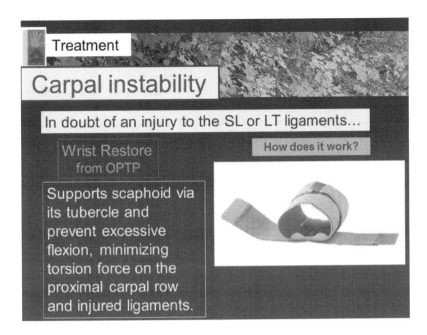

Picture 440: Slide41

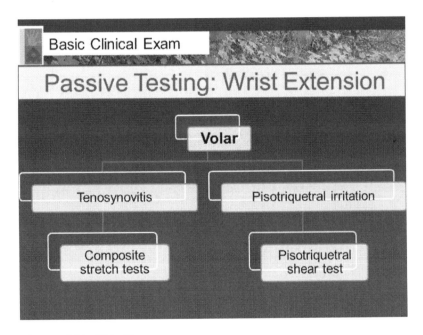

Picture 441: Slide42

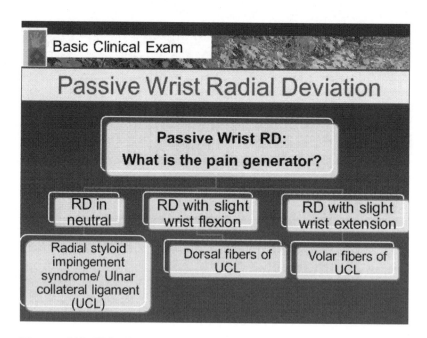

Picture 442: Slide43

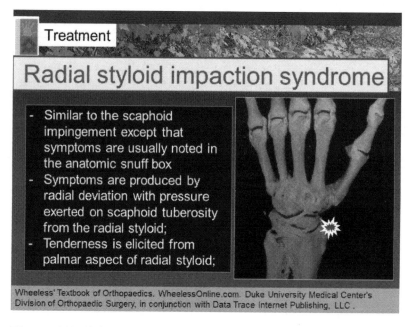

Picture 443: Slide44

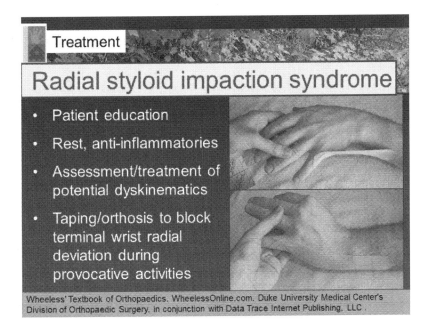

Picture 444: Slide45

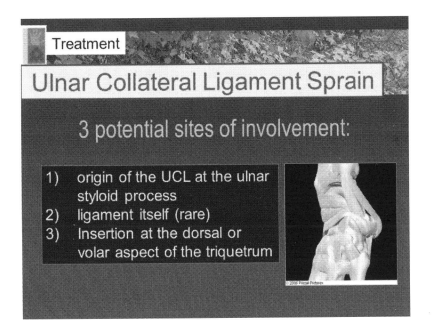

Picture 445: Slide46

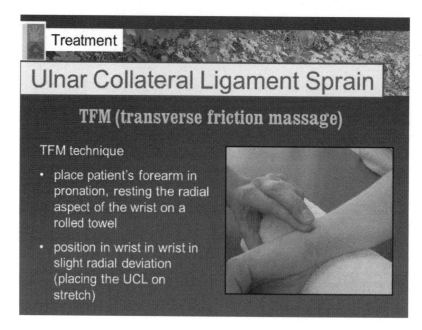

Picture 446: Slide47

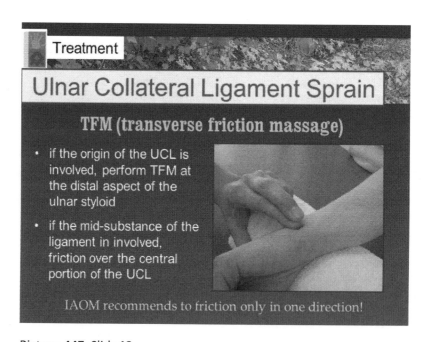

Picture 447: Slide48

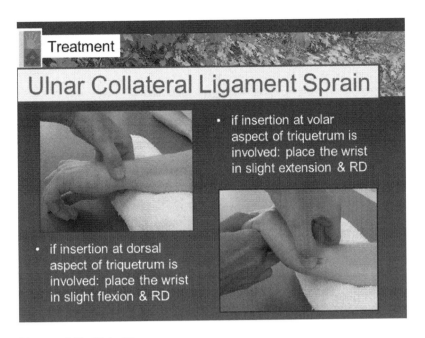

Picture 448: Slide49

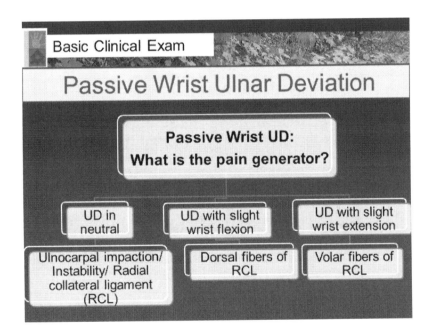

Picture 449: Slide50

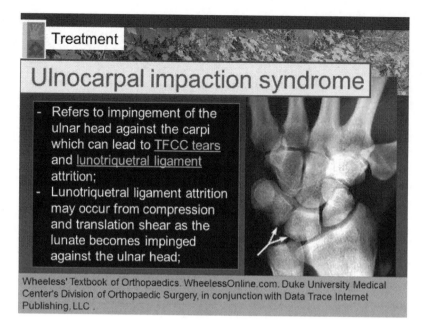

Picture 450: Slide51

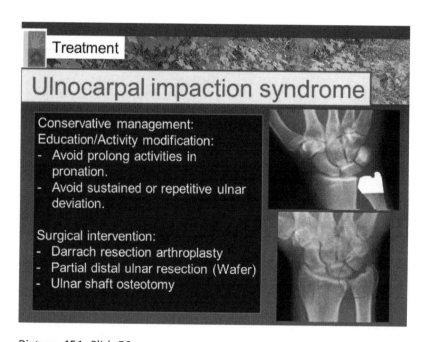

Picture 451: Slide52

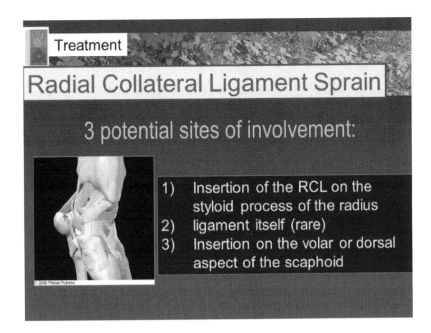

Picture 452: Slide53

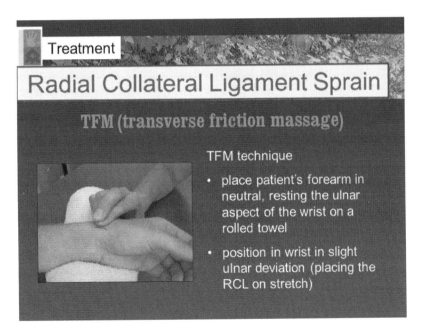

Picture 453: Slide54

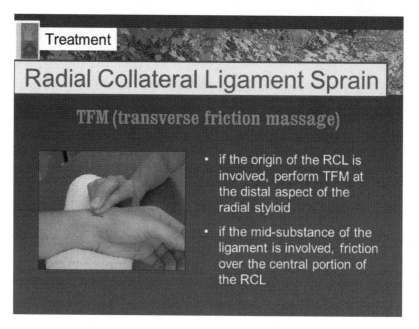

Picture 454: Slide55

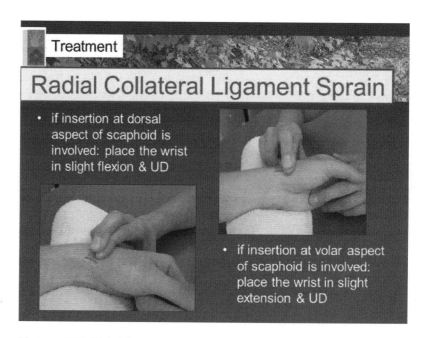

Picture 455: Slide56

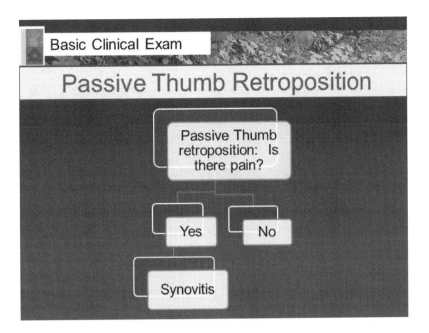

Picture 456: Slide57

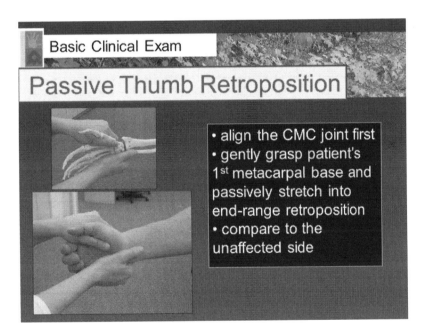

Picture 457: Slide58

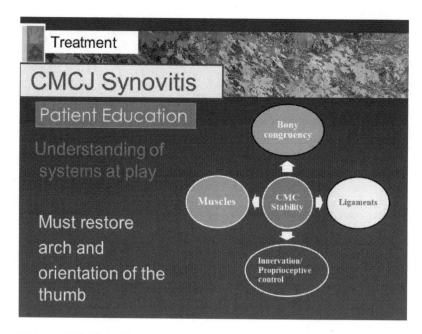

Picture 458: Slide59

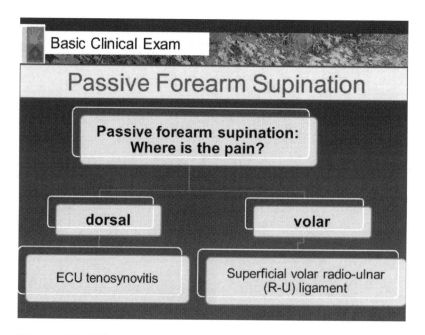

Picture 459: Slide60

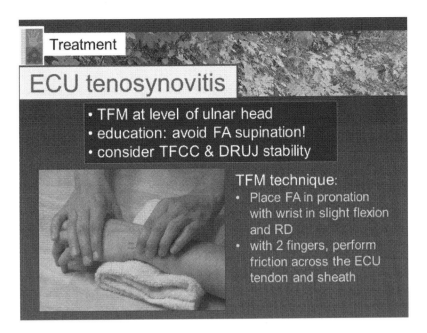

Picture 460: Slide61

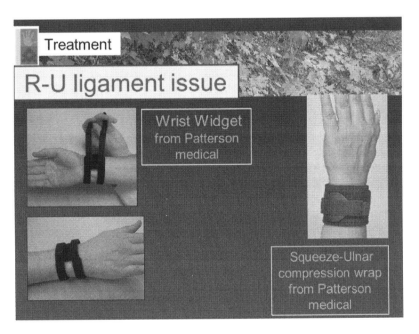

Picture 461: Slide62

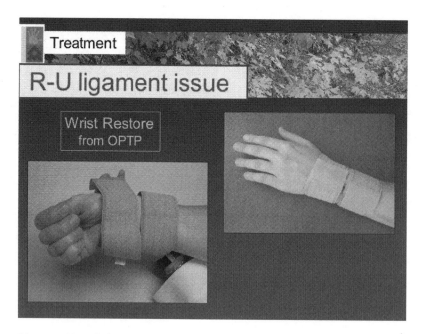

Picture 462: Slide63

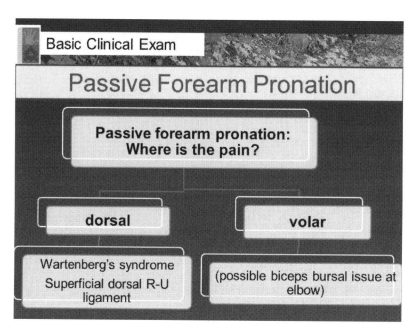

Picture 463: Slide64

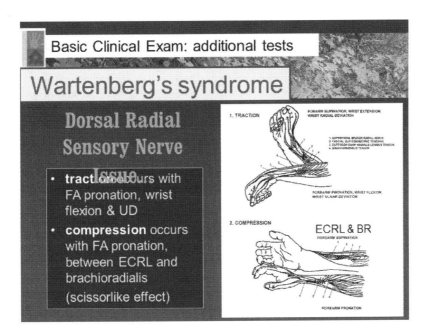

Picture 464: Slide65

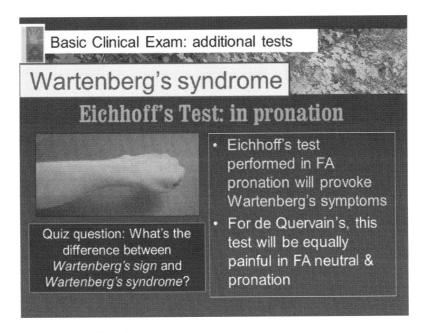

Picture 465: Slide66

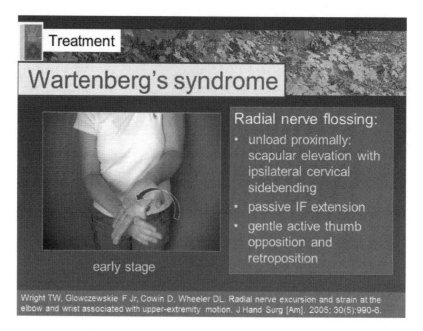

Picture 466: Slide67

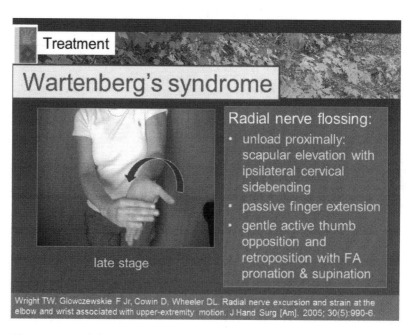

Picture 467: Slide68

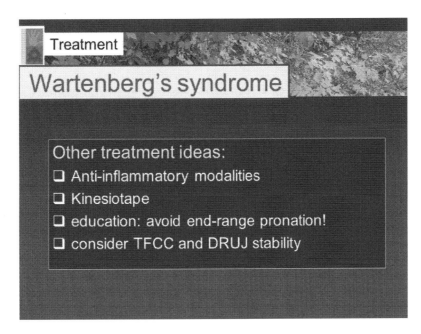

Picture 468: Slide69

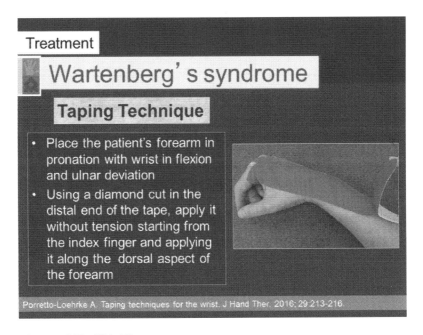

Picture 469: Slide70

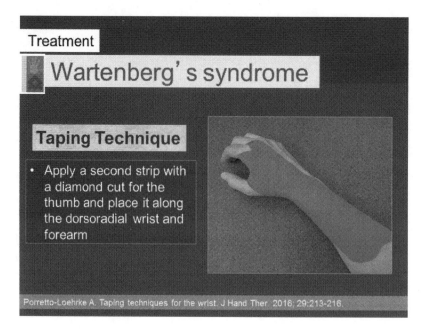

Picture 470: Slide71

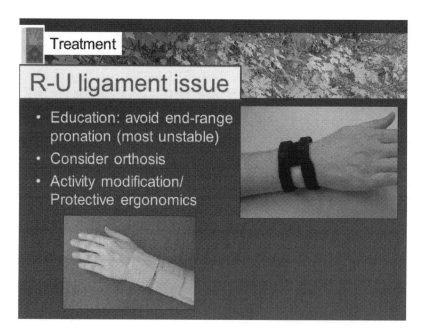

Picture 471: Slide72

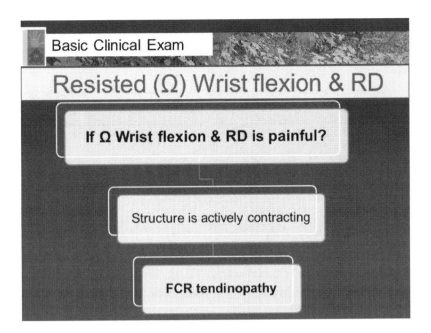

Picture 472: Slide73

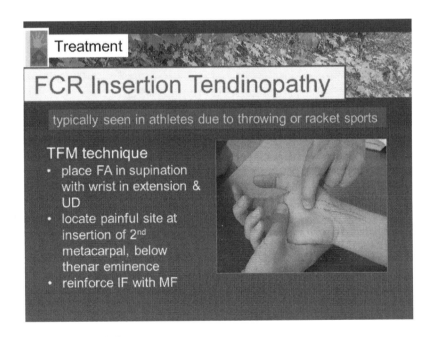

Picture 473: Slide74

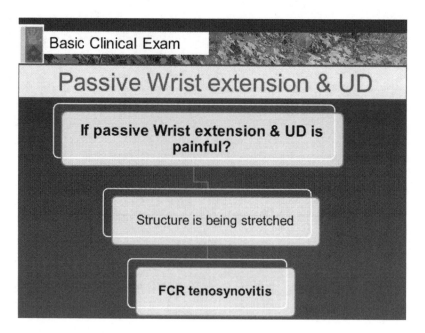

Picture 474: Slide75

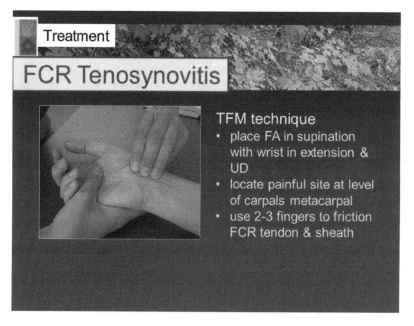

Picture 475: Slide76

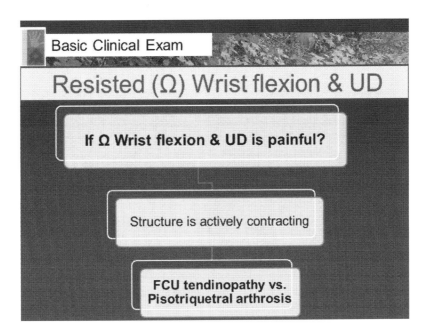

Picture 476: Slide77

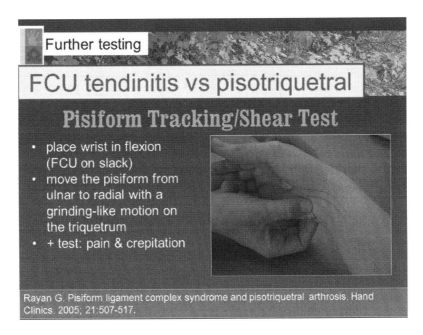

Picture 477: Slide78

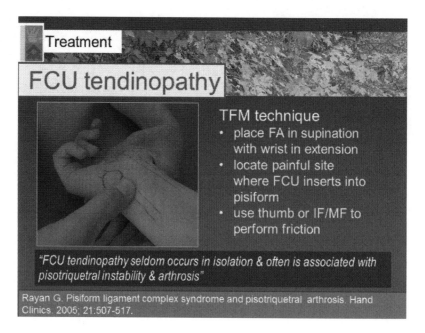

Picture 478: Slide79

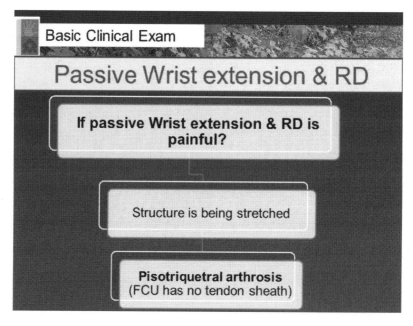

Picture 479: Slide80

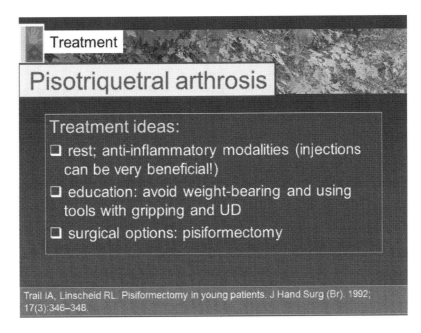

Picture 480: Slide81

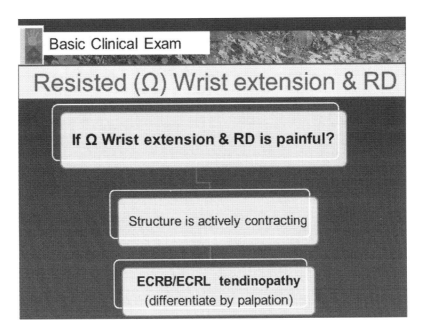

Picture 481: Slide82

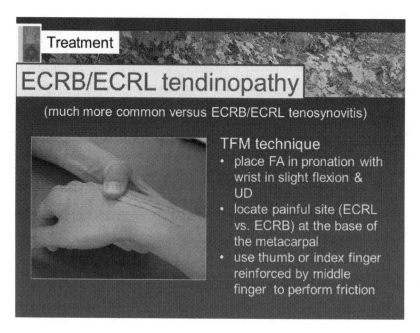

Picture 482: Slide83

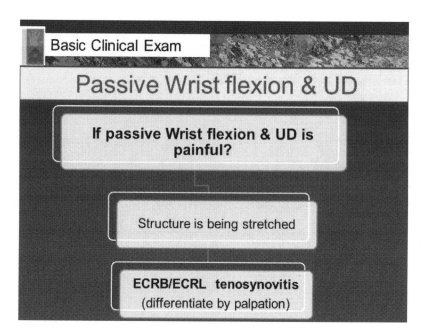

Picture 483: Slide84

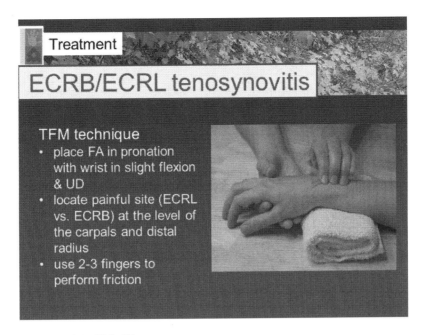

Picture 484: Slide85

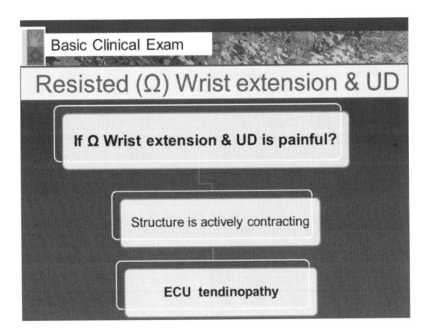

Picture 485: Slide86

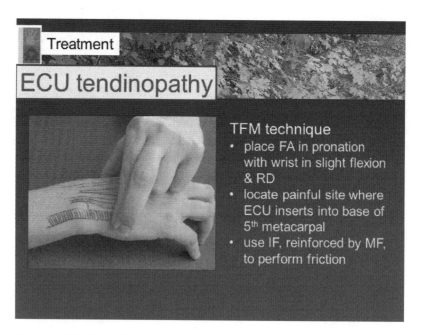

Picture 486: Slide87

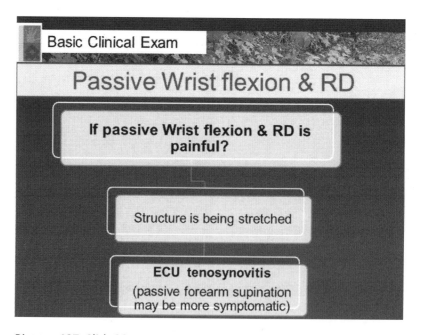

Picture 487: Slide88

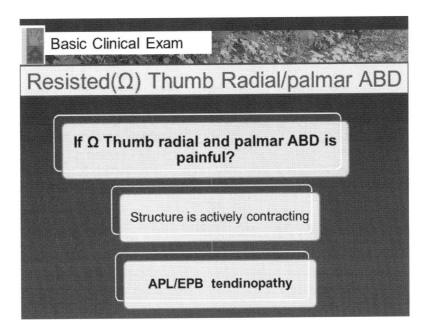

Picture 488: Slide89

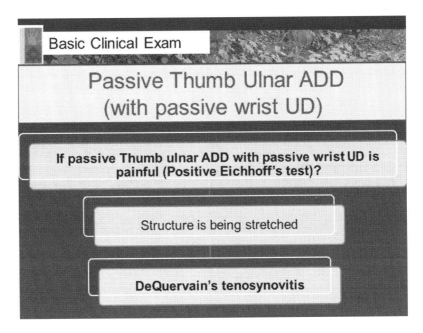

Picture 489: Slide90

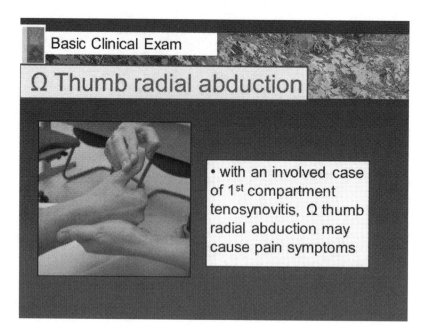

Picture 490: Slide91

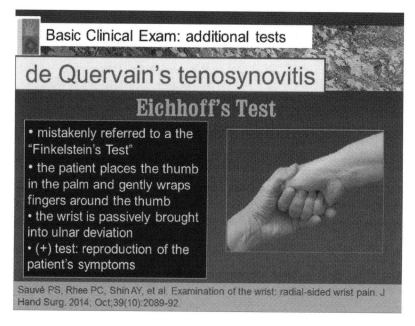

Picture 491: Slide92

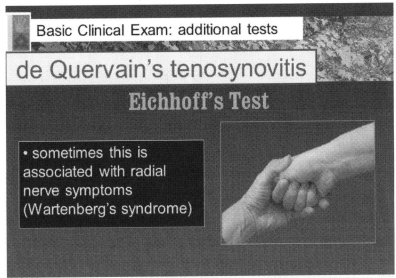

Lanzetta M, Foucher G. Association of wartenberg's syndrome and de quervain's disease: a series of 26 cases. Plastic & Reconstructive Surgery. 1995; 96(2):408-12.

Picture 492: Slide93

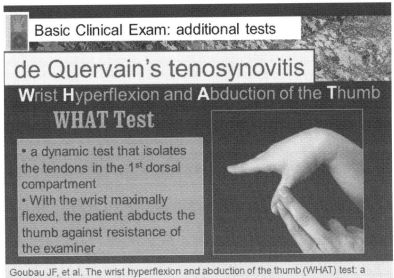

Goubau JF, et al. The wrist hyperflexion and abduction of the thumb (WHAT) test: a more specific and sensitive test to diagnose de quervain tenosynovitis than the eichhoff's test. J Hand Surg (Eur). 2014; Mar;39(3):286-92.

Picture 493: Slide94

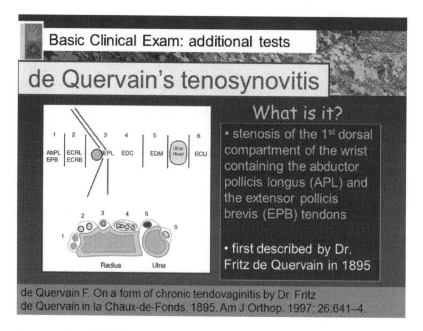

Picture 494: Slide95

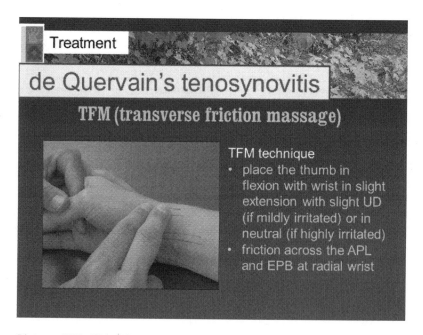

Picture 495: Slide96

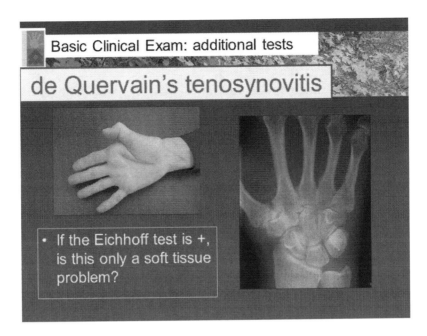

Picture 496: Slide97

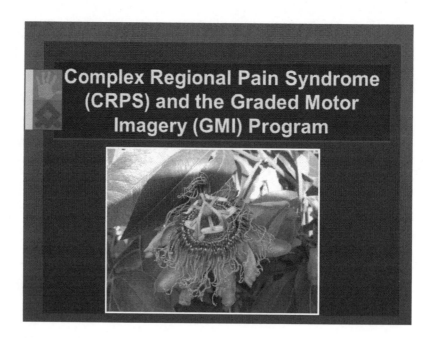

Picture 497: Slide1

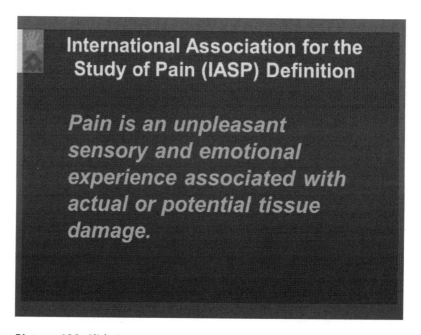

Picture 498: Slide2

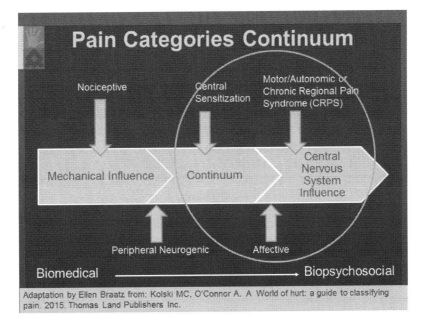

Picture 499: Slide3

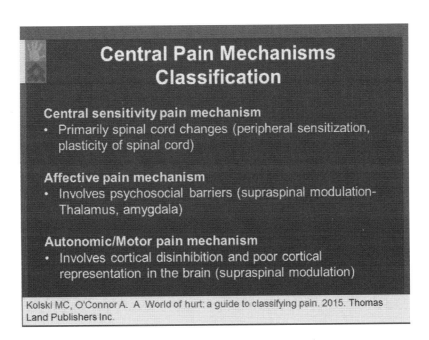

Picture 500: Slide4

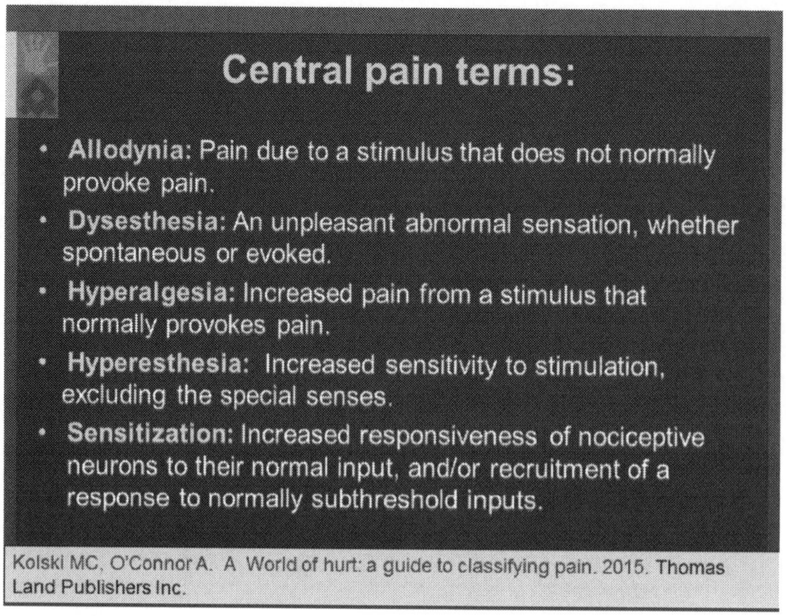

Picture 501: Slide5

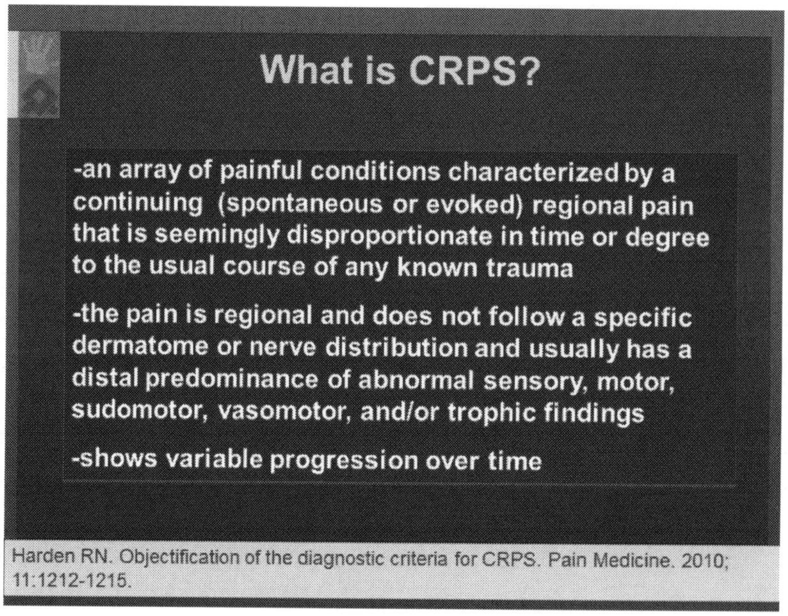

Picture 502: Slide6

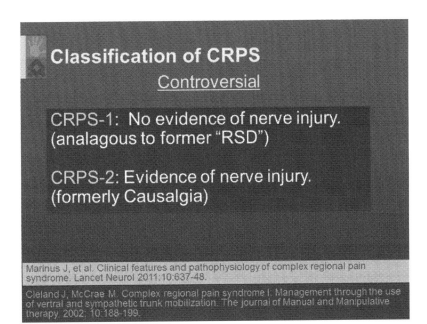

Classification of CRPS
Controversial

CRPS-1: No evidence of nerve injury.
(analagous to former "RSD")

CRPS-2: Evidence of nerve injury.
(formerly Causalgia)

Marinus J, et al. Clinical features and pathophysiology of complex regional pain syndrome. Lancet Neurol 2011;10:637-48.
Cleland J, McCrae M. Complex regional pain syndrome I: Management through the use of vertral and sympathetic trunk mobilization. The journal of Manual and Manipulative therapy. 2002; 10:188-199.

Picture 503: Slide7

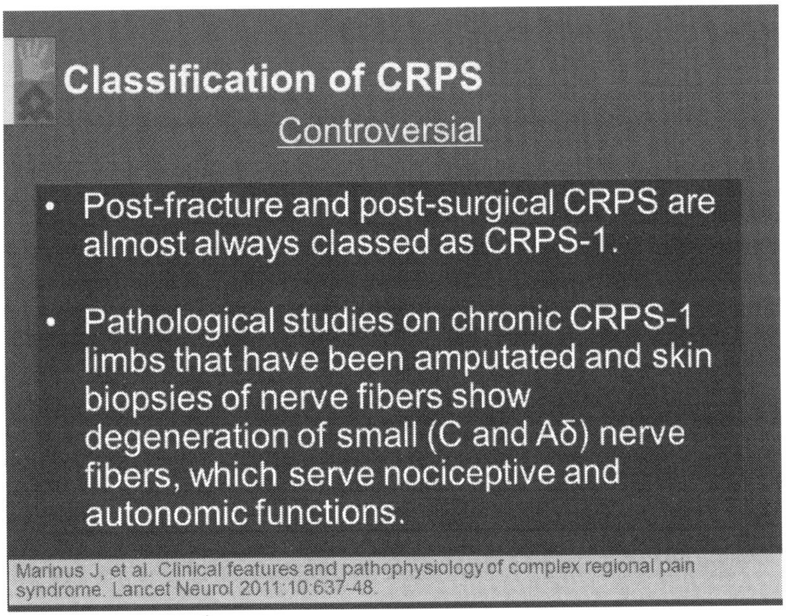

Classification of CRPS
Controversial

- Post-fracture and post-surgical CRPS are almost always classed as CRPS-1.

- Pathological studies on chronic CRPS-1 limbs that have been amputated and skin biopsies of nerve fibers show degeneration of small (C and Aδ) nerve fibers, which serve nociceptive and autonomic functions.

Marinus J, et al. Clinical features and pathophysiology of complex regional pain syndrome. Lancet Neurol 2011;10:637-48.

Picture 504: Slide8

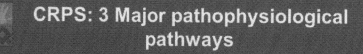

CRPS: 3 Major pathophysiological pathways

- Aberrant inflammatory mechanism
- Vasomotor dysfunction
- Maladaptive neuroplasticity

The clinical heterogeneity of CRPS is indicative of **between-individual variability** in the activation of these pathways after tissue injury.

Marinus J, et al. Clinical features and pathophysiology of complex regional pain syndrome. Lancet Neurol 2011:10:637-48.

Picture 505: Slide9

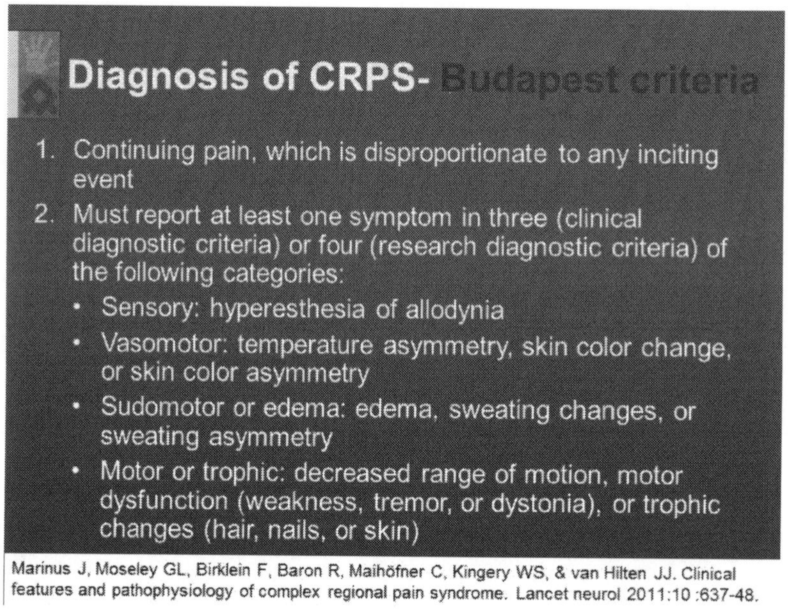

Diagnosis of CRPS- Budapest criteria

1. Continuing pain, which is disproportionate to any inciting event
2. Must report at least one symptom in three (clinical diagnostic criteria) or four (research diagnostic criteria) of the following categories:
   - Sensory: hyperesthesia of allodynia
   - Vasomotor: temperature asymmetry, skin color change, or skin color asymmetry
   - Sudomotor or edema: edema, sweating changes, or sweating asymmetry
   - Motor or trophic: decreased range of motion, motor dysfunction (weakness, tremor, or dystonia), or trophic changes (hair, nails, or skin)

Marinus J, Moseley GL, Birklein F, Baron R, Maihöfner C, Kingery WS, & van Hilten JJ. Clinical features and pathophysiology of complex regional pain syndrome. Lancet neurol 2011:10 :637-48.

Picture 506: Slide10

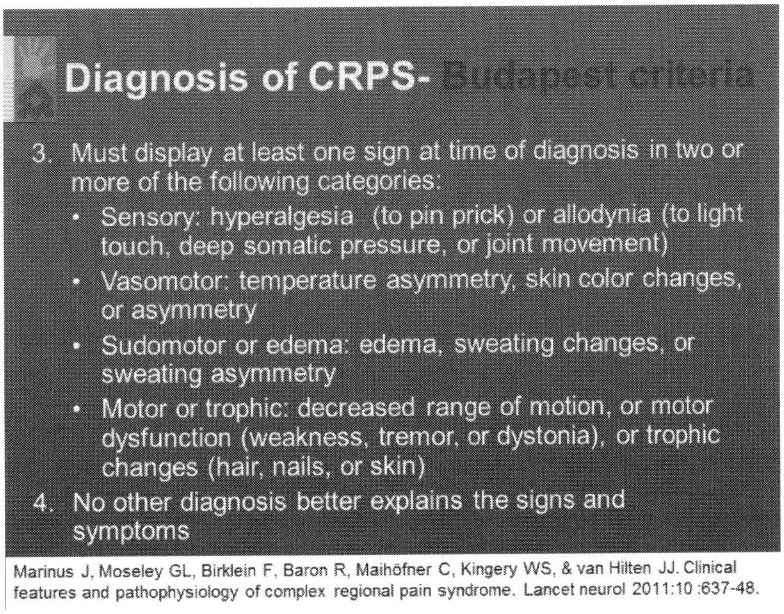

Diagnosis of CRPS- Budapest criteria

3. Must display at least one sign at time of diagnosis in two or more of the following categories:
   - Sensory: hyperalgesia (to pin prick) or allodynia (to light touch, deep somatic pressure, or joint movement)
   - Vasomotor: temperature asymmetry, skin color changes, or asymmetry
   - Sudomotor or edema: edema, sweating changes, or sweating asymmetry
   - Motor or trophic: decreased range of motion, or motor dysfunction (weakness, tremor, or dystonia), or trophic changes (hair, nails, or skin)
4. No other diagnosis better explains the signs and symptoms

Marinus J, Moseley GL, Birklein F, Baron R, Maihöfner C, Kingery WS, & van Hilten JJ. Clinical features and pathophysiology of complex regional pain syndrome. Lancet neurol 2011:10 :637-48.

Picture 507: Slide11

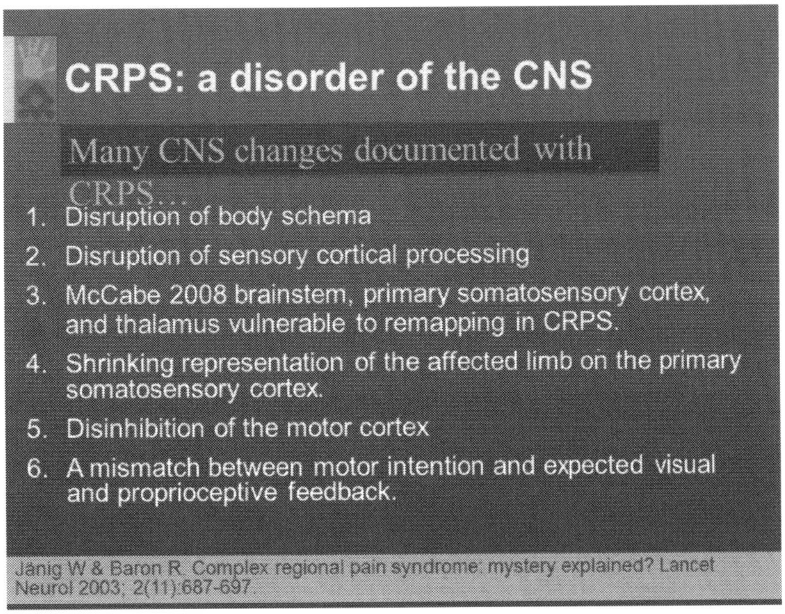

CRPS: a disorder of the CNS

Many CNS changes documented with CRPS...

1. Disruption of body schema
2. Disruption of sensory cortical processing
3. McCabe 2008 brainstem, primary somatosensory cortex, and thalamus vulnerable to remapping in CRPS.
4. Shrinking representation of the affected limb on the primary somatosensory cortex.
5. Disinhibition of the motor cortex
6. A mismatch between motor intention and expected visual and proprioceptive feedback.

Jänig W & Baron R. Complex regional pain syndrome: mystery explained? Lancet Neurol 2003; 2(11):687-697.

Picture 508: Slide12

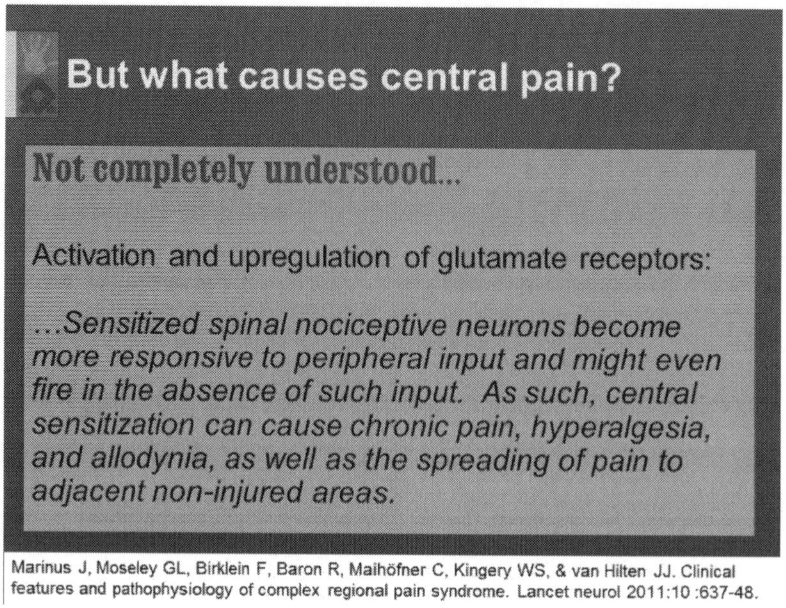

But what causes central pain?

Not completely understood...

Activation and upregulation of glutamate receptors:

...Sensitized spinal nociceptive neurons become more responsive to peripheral input and might even fire in the absence of such input. As such, central sensitization can cause chronic pain, hyperalgesia, and allodynia, as well as the spreading of pain to adjacent non-injured areas.

Marinus J, Moseley GL, Birklein F, Baron R, Maihöfner C, Kingery WS, & van Hilten JJ. Clinical features and pathophysiology of complex regional pain syndrome. Lancet neurol 2011:10 :637-48.

Picture 509: Slide13

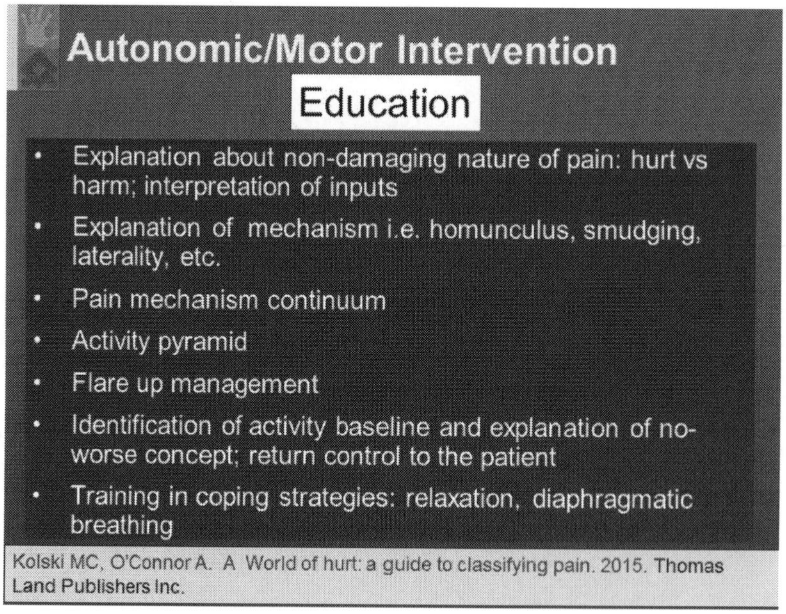

Autonomic/Motor Intervention
Education

- Explanation about non-damaging nature of pain: hurt vs harm; interpretation of inputs
- Explanation of mechanism i.e. homunculus, smudging, laterality, etc.
- Pain mechanism continuum
- Activity pyramid
- Flare up management
- Identification of activity baseline and explanation of no-worse concept; return control to the patient
- Training in coping strategies: relaxation, diaphragmatic breathing

Kolski MC, O'Connor A. A World of hurt: a guide to classifying pain. 2015. Thomas Land Publishers Inc.

Picture 510: Slide14

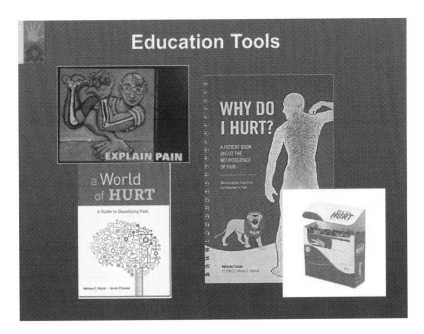

Picture 511: Slide15

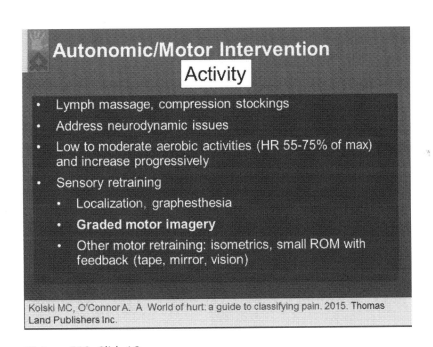

Picture 512: Slide16

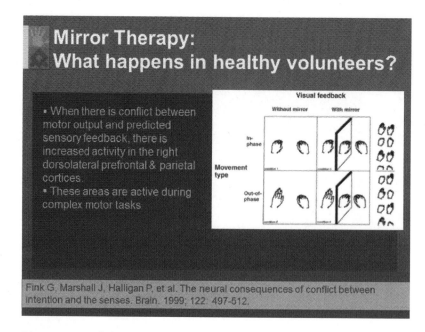

Picture 513: Slide17

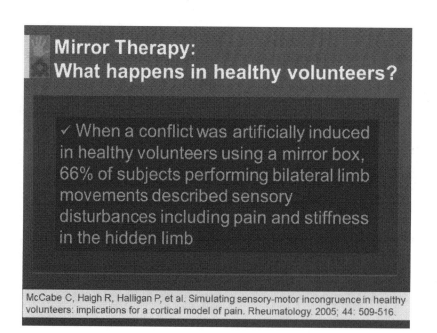

Picture 514: Slide18

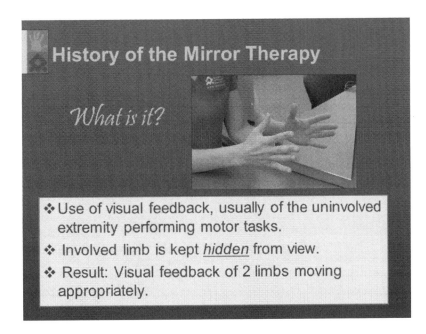

History of the Mirror Therapy

What is it?

❖ Use of visual feedback, usually of the uninvolved extremity performing motor tasks.

❖ Involved limb is kept _hidden_ from view.

❖ Result: Visual feedback of 2 limbs moving appropriately.

Picture 515: Slide19

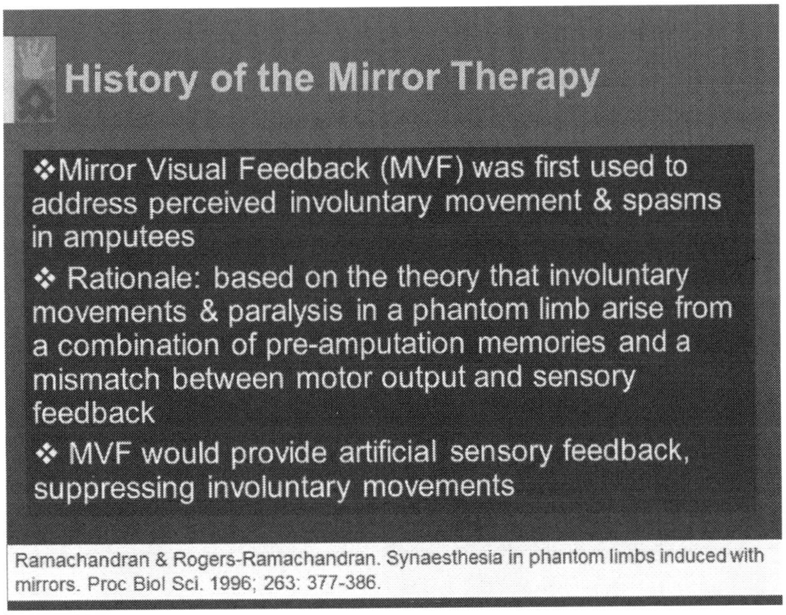

History of the Mirror Therapy

❖ Mirror Visual Feedback (MVF) was first used to address perceived involuntary movement & spasms in amputees

❖ Rationale: based on the theory that involuntary movements & paralysis in a phantom limb arise from a combination of pre-amputation memories and a mismatch between motor output and sensory feedback

❖ MVF would provide artificial sensory feedback, suppressing involuntary movements

Ramachandran & Rogers-Ramachandran. Synaesthesia in phantom limbs induced with mirrors. Proc Biol Sci. 1996; 263: 377-386.

Picture 516: Slide20

History of the Mirror Therapy

❖ the experiment set out to improve motor control of a phantom limb....however, it provided pain relief instead!

❖ One patient described a permanent disappearance of phantom limb pain after using the mirror box for 10 minutes per day for 10 weeks

Ramachandran & Rogers-Ramachandran. Synaesthesia in phantom limbs induced with mirrors. Proc Biol Sci. 1996; 263: 377-386.

Picture 517: Slide21

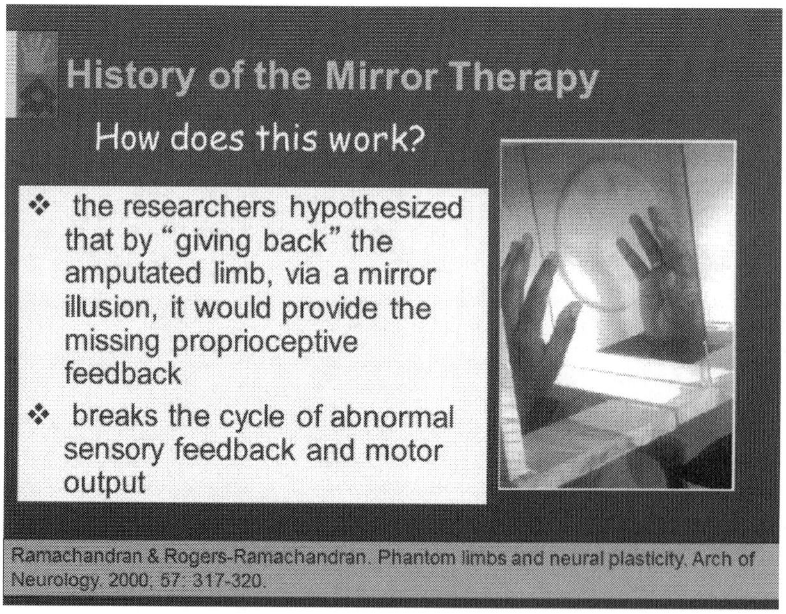

History of the Mirror Therapy

How does this work?

❖ the researchers hypothesized that by "giving back" the amputated limb, via a mirror illusion, it would provide the missing proprioceptive feedback

❖ breaks the cycle of abnormal sensory feedback and motor output

Ramachandran & Rogers-Ramachandran. Phantom limbs and neural plasticity. Arch of Neurology. 2000; 57: 317-320.

Picture 518: Slide22

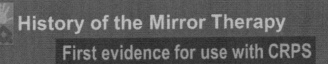

History of the Mirror Therapy
First evidence for use with CRPS

○Mirror therapy has been shown to be effective in phantom limb pain and stroke

○CRPS patients with symptom onset < 8 weeks had immediate temporary pain relief with use of mirror (n=3) After 6 weeks normal skin temp, painfree, normal function

○However, patient's with CRPS > 2 years actually had increased pain with mirror therapy

○Hypothesized to be effective by re-establishment of normal pain-free relationship between sensory feedback and motor intention

McCabe, CS, et al. A controlled pilot study of the utility of mirror visual feedback in the treatment of complex regional pain syndrome. Rheumatology. 2003;43:97-101.

Picture 519: Slide23

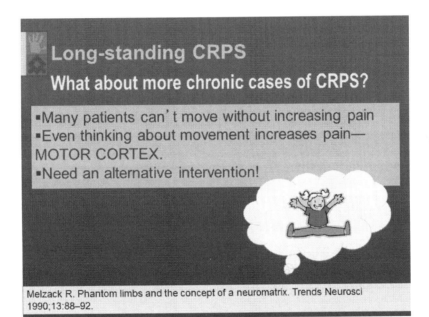

Long-standing CRPS
What about more chronic cases of CRPS?

▪Many patients can't move without increasing pain
▪Even thinking about movement increases pain— MOTOR CORTEX.
▪Need an alternative intervention!

Melzack R. Phantom limbs and the concept of a neuromatrix. Trends Neurosci 1990;13:88–92.

Picture 520: Slide24

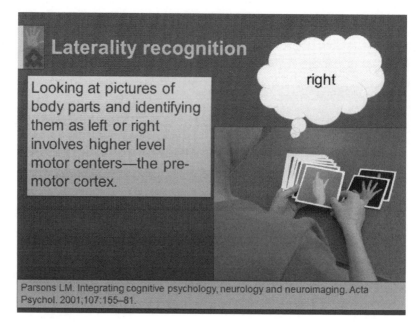

Picture 521: Slide25

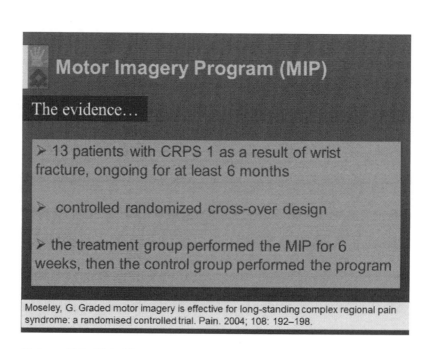

Picture 522: Slide26

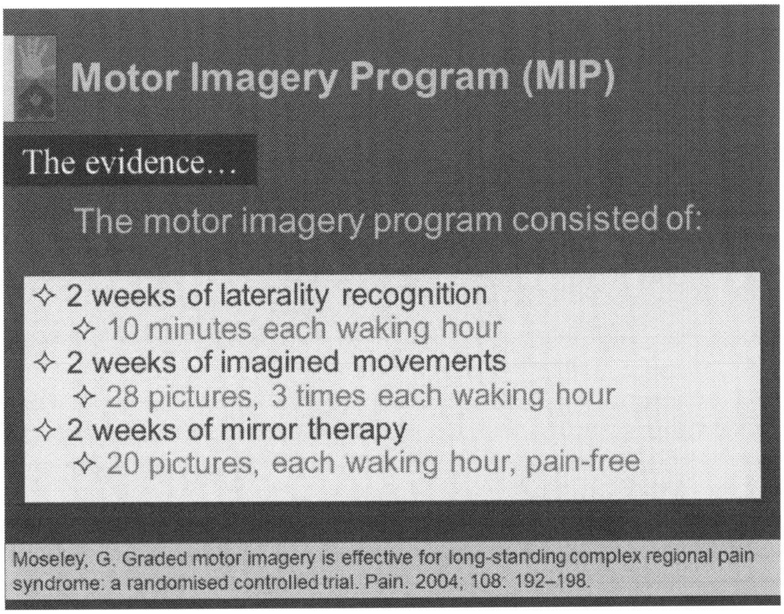

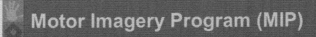

Motor Imagery Program (MIP)

The evidence...

The motor imagery program consisted of:

- ✧ 2 weeks of laterality recognition
  - ✧ 10 minutes each waking hour
- ✧ 2 weeks of imagined movements
  - ✧ 28 pictures, 3 times each waking hour
- ✧ 2 weeks of mirror therapy
  - ✧ 20 pictures, each waking hour, pain-free

Moseley, G. Graded motor imagery is effective for long-standing complex regional pain syndrome: a randomised controlled trial. Pain. 2004; 108: 192–198.

Picture 523: Slide27

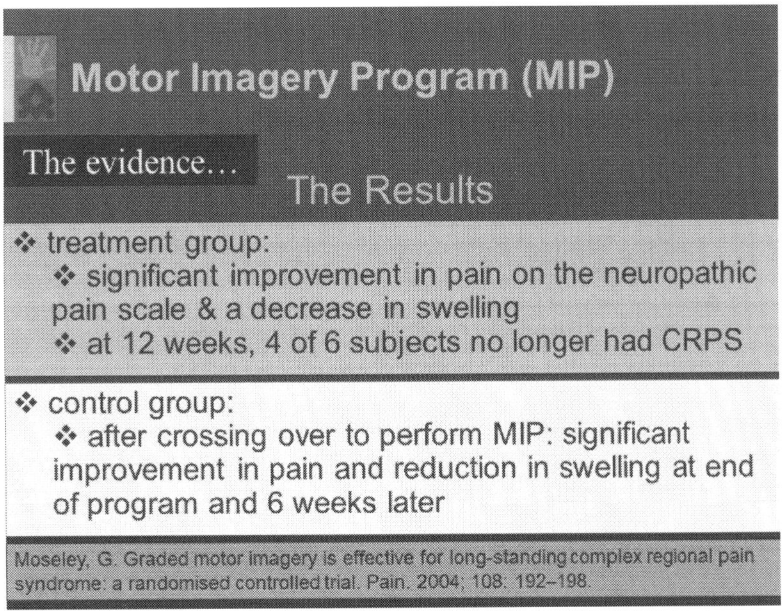

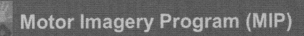

Motor Imagery Program (MIP)

The evidence... The Results

- ❖ treatment group:
  - ❖ significant improvement in pain on the neuropathic pain scale & a decrease in swelling
  - ❖ at 12 weeks, 4 of 6 subjects no longer had CRPS

- ❖ control group:
  - ❖ after crossing over to perform MIP: significant improvement in pain and reduction in swelling at end of program and 6 weeks later

Moseley, G. Graded motor imagery is effective for long-standing complex regional pain syndrome: a randomised controlled trial. Pain. 2004; 108: 192–198.

Picture 524: Slide28

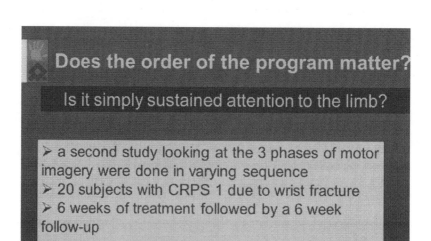

Picture 525: Slide29

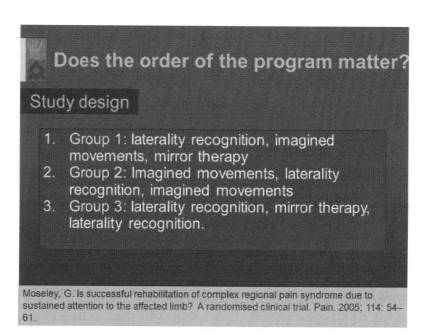

Picture 526: Slide30

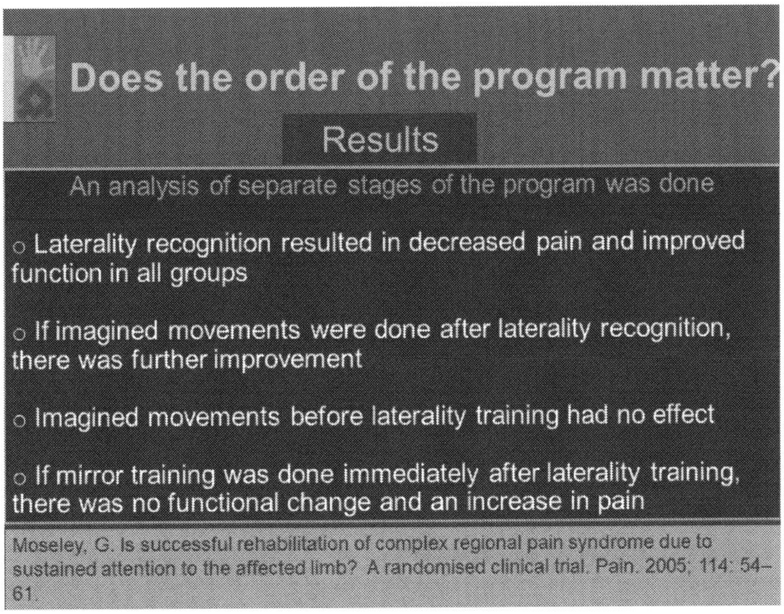

Does the order of the program matter?

Results

An analysis of separate stages of the program was done

o Laterality recognition resulted in decreased pain and improved function in all groups

o If imagined movements were done after laterality recognition, there was further improvement

o Imagined movements before laterality training had no effect

o If mirror training was done immediately after laterality training, there was no functional change and an increase in pain

Moseley, G. Is successful rehabilitation of complex regional pain syndrome due to sustained attention to the affected limb? A randomised clinical trial. Pain. 2005; 114: 54–61.

Picture 527: Slide31

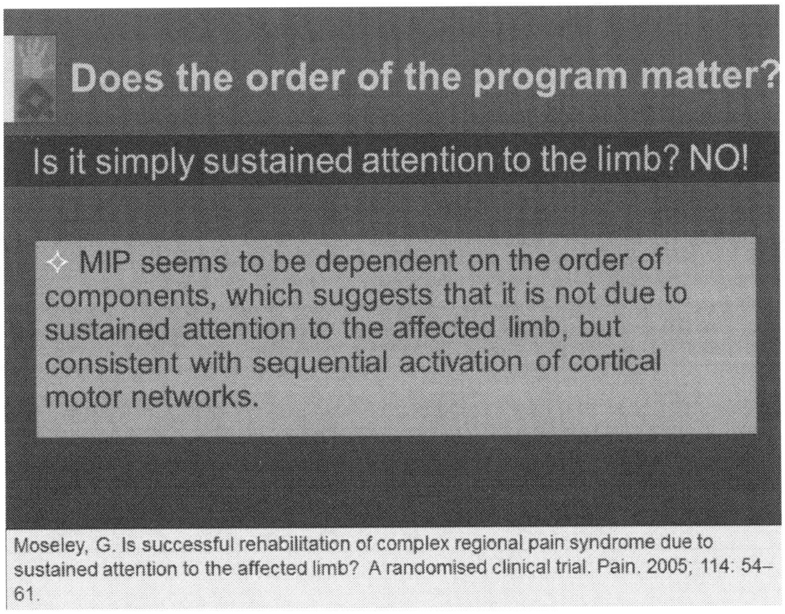

Does the order of the program matter?

Is it simply sustained attention to the limb? NO!

◇ MIP seems to be dependent on the order of components, which suggests that it is not due to sustained attention to the affected limb, but consistent with sequential activation of cortical motor networks.

Moseley, G. Is successful rehabilitation of complex regional pain syndrome due to sustained attention to the affected limb? A randomised clinical trial. Pain. 2005; 114: 54–61.

Picture 528: Slide32

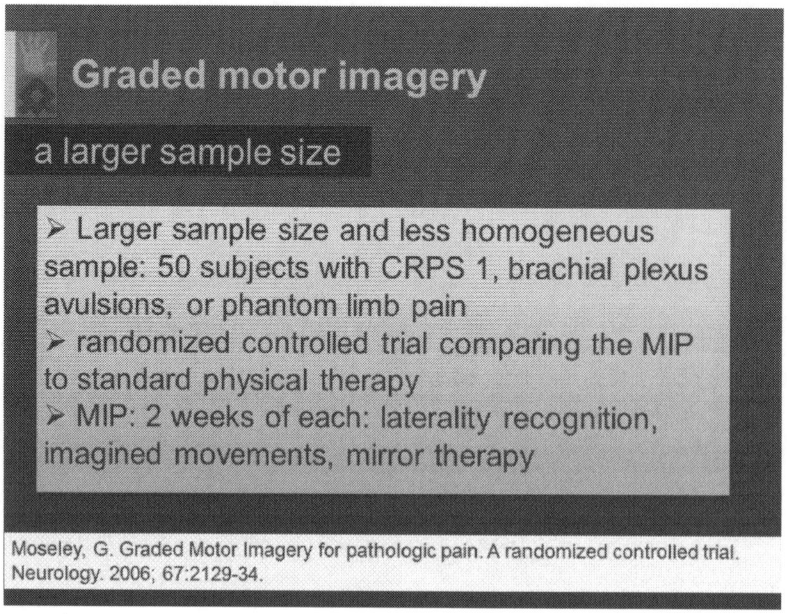

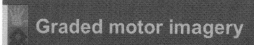

Graded motor imagery

a larger sample size

> Larger sample size and less homogeneous sample: 50 subjects with CRPS 1, brachial plexus avulsions, or phantom limb pain
> randomized controlled trial comparing the MIP to standard physical therapy
> MIP: 2 weeks of each: laterality recognition, imagined movements, mirror therapy

Moseley, G. Graded Motor Imagery for pathologic pain. A randomized controlled trial. Neurology. 2006; 67:2129-34.

Picture 529: Slide33

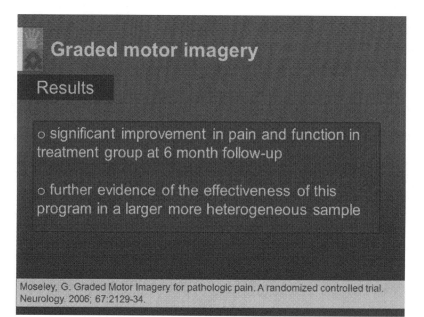

Graded motor imagery

Results

o significant improvement in pain and function in treatment group at 6 month follow-up

o further evidence of the effectiveness of this program in a larger more heterogeneous sample

Moseley, G. Graded Motor Imagery for pathologic pain. A randomized controlled trial. Neurology. 2006; 67:2129-34.

Picture 530: Slide34

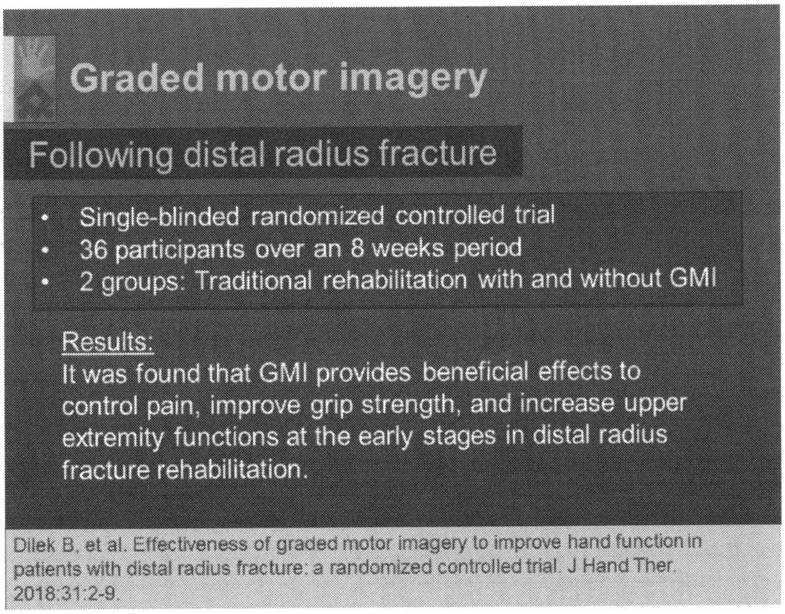

Picture 531: Slide35

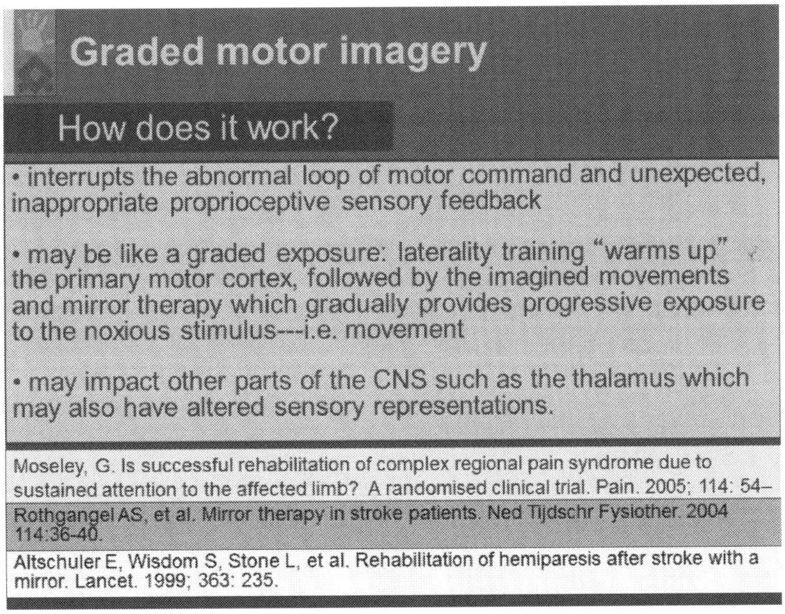

Picture 532: Slide36

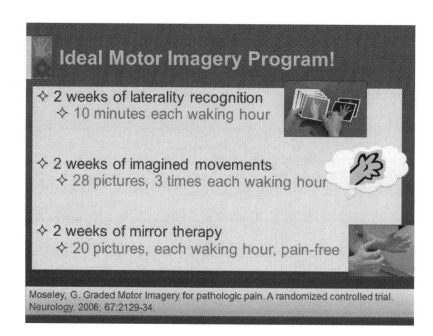

Picture 533: Slide37

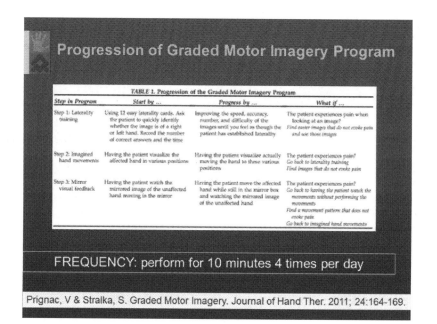

Picture 534: Slide38

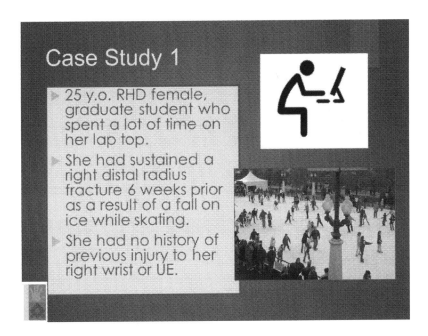

Picture 535: Slide1

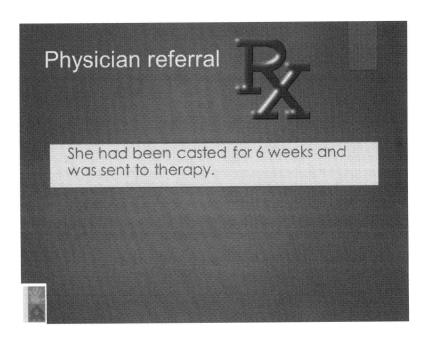

Picture 536: Slide2

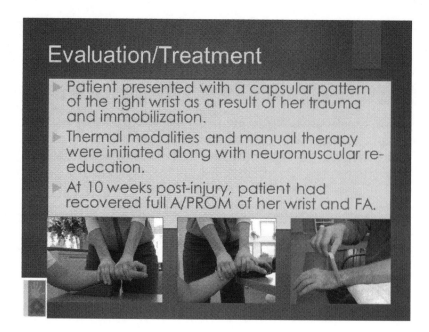

Picture 537: Slide3

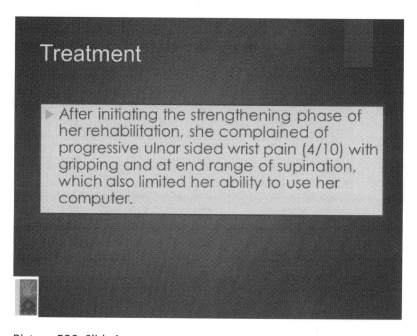

Picture 538: Slide4

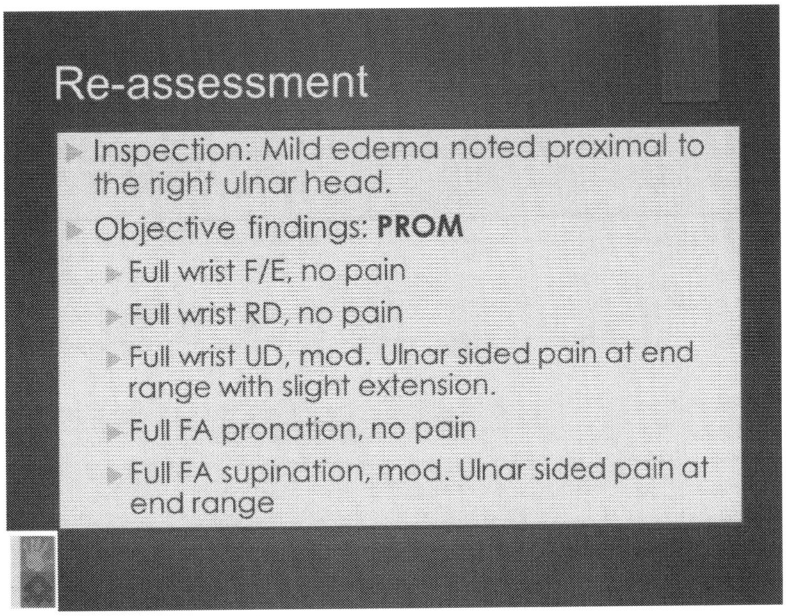

Re-assessment

- Inspection: Mild edema noted proximal to the right ulnar head.
- Objective findings: **PROM**
  - Full wrist F/E, no pain
  - Full wrist RD, no pain
  - Full wrist UD, mod. Ulnar sided pain at end range with slight extension.
  - Full FA pronation, no pain
  - Full FA supination, mod. Ulnar sided pain at end range

Picture 539: Slide5

Re-assessment

- Objective findings: **MMT**
  - Resisted wrist extension with UD: mild ulnar sided pain
  - Passive wrist flexion with RD: mod. Ulnar sided pain
- Special test:
  - ECU synergy test: mod. Pain
- Palpation: Tenderness of ECU tendon and sheath

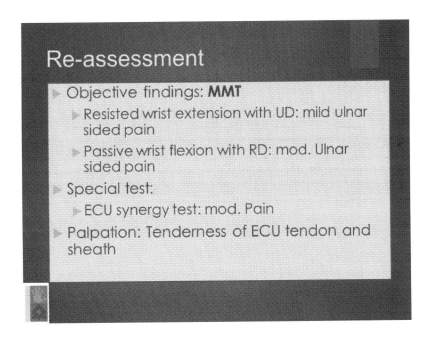

Picture 540: Slide6

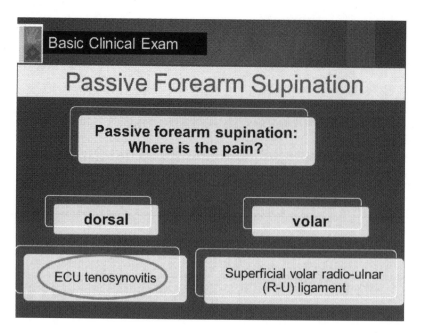

Picture 541: Slide7

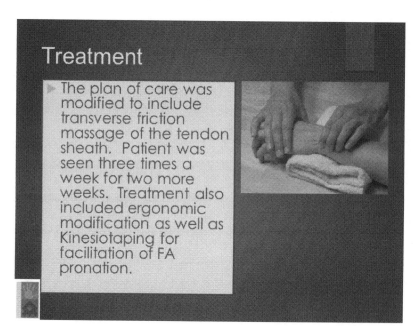

Picture 542: Slide8

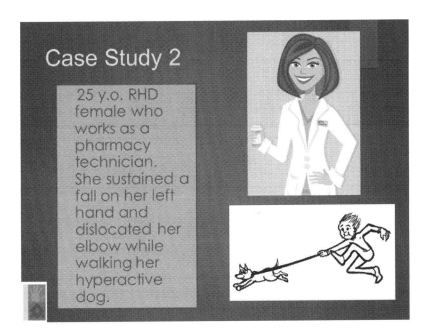

Picture 543: Slide9

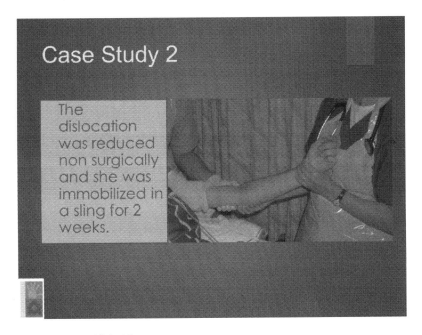

Picture 544: Slide10

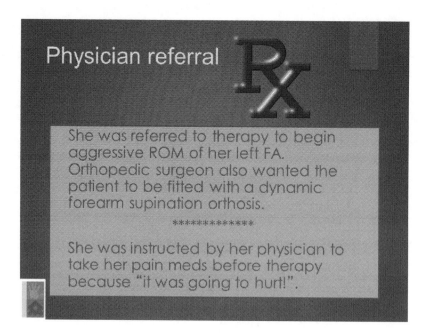

Picture 545: Slide11

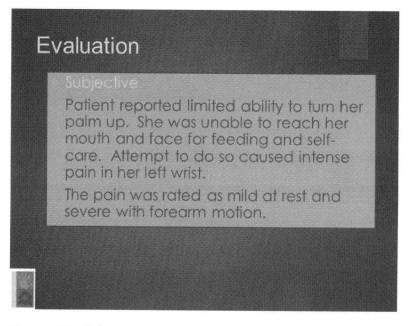

Picture 546: Slide12

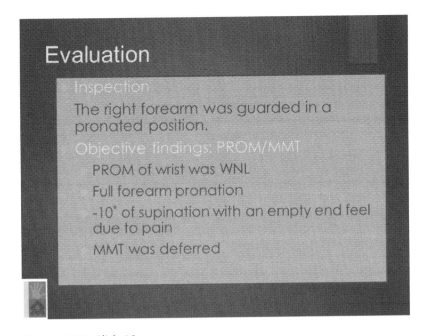

Picture 547: Slide13

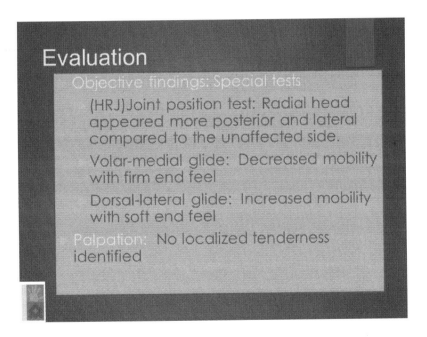

Picture 548: Slide14

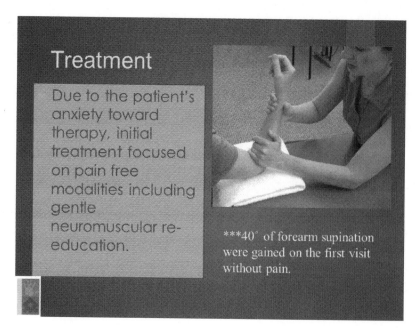

Picture 549: Slide15

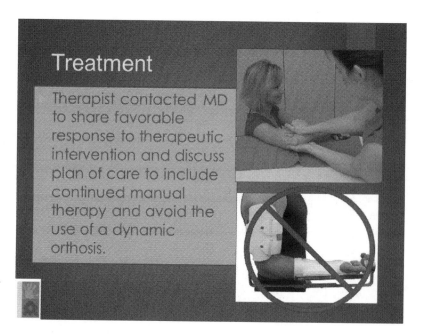

Picture 550: Slide16

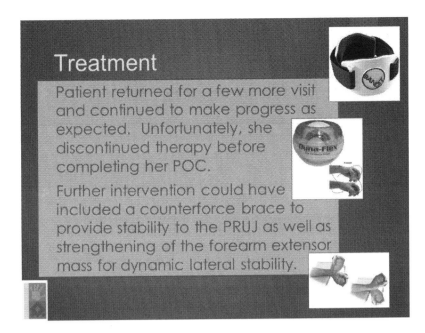

Picture 551: Slide17

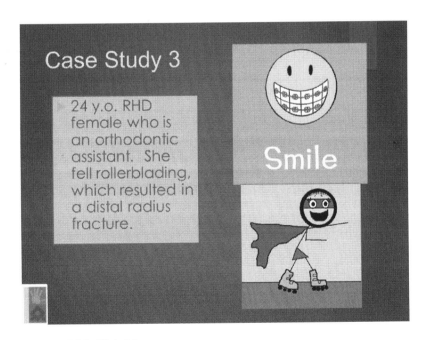

Picture 552: Slide18

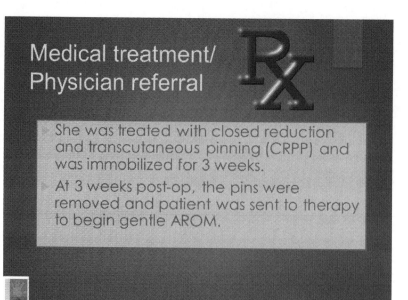

Medical treatment/ Physician referral

She was treated with closed reduction and transcutaneous pinning (CRPP) and was immobilized for 3 weeks.

At 3 weeks post-op, the pins were removed and patient was sent to therapy to begin gentle AROM.

Picture 553: Slide19

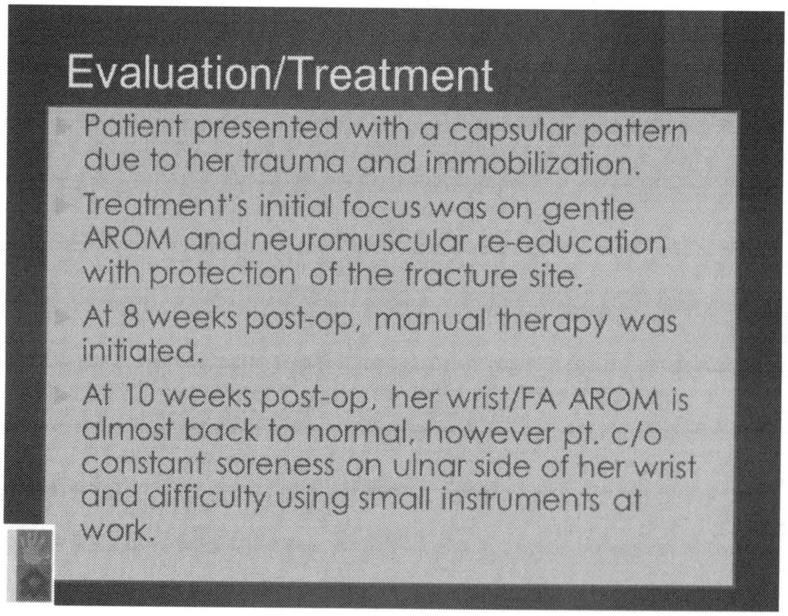

Evaluation/Treatment

Patient presented with a capsular pattern due to her trauma and immobilization.

Treatment's initial focus was on gentle AROM and neuromuscular re-education with protection of the fracture site.

At 8 weeks post-op, manual therapy was initiated.

At 10 weeks post-op, her wrist/FA AROM is almost back to normal, however pt. c/o constant soreness on ulnar side of her wrist and difficulty using small instruments at work.

Picture 554: Slide20

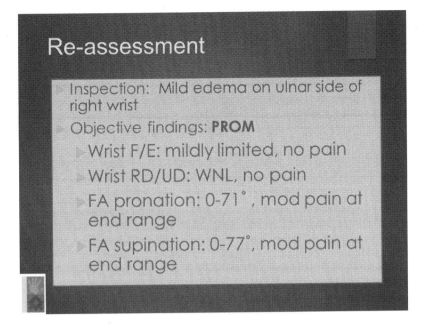

Picture 555: Slide21

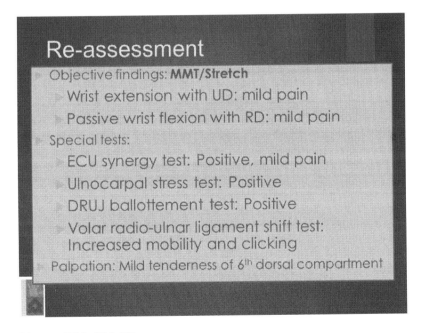

Picture 556: Slide22

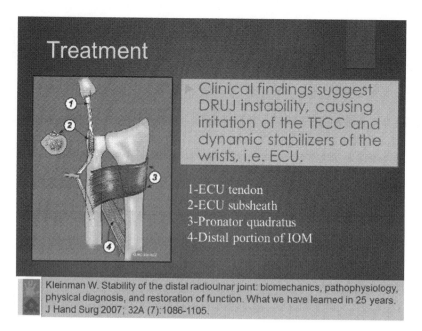

Picture 557: Slide23

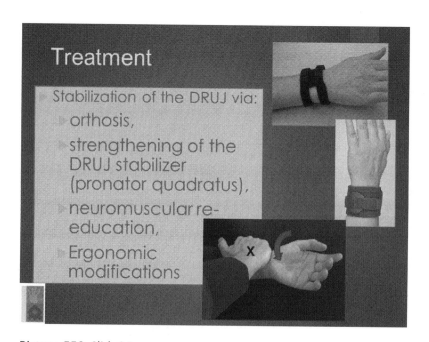

Picture 558: Slide24

Picture 559: Slide25

Differential Diagnosis & Manual Therapy of the Wrist—Level I

1. Acosta R, Hnat W, Scheker LR. Distal radio-ulnar ligament motion during pronation and supination. J Hand Surg (Br). 1993; 18B: 502-505

2. Adams JE. Forearm instability: anatomy, biomechanics, and treatment options. J Hand Surg Am. 2017; 42(1):47-52.

3. Altman E. The ulnar side of the wrist: clinically relevant anatomy and biomechanics. J Hand Ther. 2016;29:111-122.

4. Amirfeyz R, Gozzard C, Leslie IJ. Hand elevation test for assessment of carpal tunnel syndrome. J Hand Surg Br. 2005; 30:361-364.

5. Berger R. (1997) The Ligaments of the Wrist. *Hand Clinics.*13; 63-82.

6. Berger RA. The anatomy of the ligaments of the wrist and distal radioulnar joints. Clin Orth Rel Res 2001; 383:32-40.

7. Berger RA, Imeada T, Berglund L, An K-N. Constraint and material properties of the subregions of the scapholunate interosseous ligament. J Hand Surg. 1999; 24A: 953-962.

8. Brantigan C & Roos D. Diagnosing thoracic outlet syndrome. Hand Clinics. 2004; 20: 27-36.

9. Brismée JM, et al. Rate of false positive using the Cyriax release test for thoracic outlet syndrome in an asymptomatic population. Journal of Manual & Manipulative Therapy. 2004; 12(2): 73-81.

10. Chidgey LK. The distal radioulnar joint: problems and solutions. J Am Acad Orthop Surg. 1995; 2: 95–109.

11. Dao KD, Shin AY. Percutaneous cannulated screw fixation of acute nondisplaced scaphoid waist fractures. Atlas of Hand Clin 9 2004; 141-148.

12. Dawson JS, Martel AL, Davis TRC. Scaphoid blood flow and acute fracture healing. J Bone Joint Surg 2001; 83-B: 809-814.

13. Dell P, Dell R. Management of Carpal Fractures and Dislocations (2002). Rehabilitation of the Hand the Upper Extremity:1171-1173.

14. de Quervain F. On a form of chronic tendovaginitis by Dr. Fritz de Quervain in la Chaux-de-Fonds. 1895. Am J Orthop. 1997; 26:641–4.

15. de Muinck Keizer RJO et al. Three dimensional virtual planning of corrective osteotomies of distal radius malunions: a systematic review and meta-analysis. Strat Traum Limb Recon (2017)12:77-89

16. Dilek B, et al. Effectiveness of graded motor imagery to improve hand function in patients with distal radius fracture: a randomized controlled trial. J Hand Ther. 2018;31:2-9.

17. Dy CJ, et al. The impact of coronal alignment on distal radioulnar joint stability following distal radius fracture. J Hand Surg Am. 2014; 39(7):1264-1272.

18. Ekenstam, FA. Anatomy of the distal radioulnar joint. Clin Orthop Rel Res. 1992; 276: 14-18.

19. Epner RA, Bower WH, Guildford WB. Ulnar variance: The effect of wrist positioning and roentgen filming technique. J Hand Surg. 1982;7:298-305.

20. Farr LD, et al. Anatomy and biomechanics of the forearm interosseous membrane. J Hand Surg Am. 2015; 40(6):1145-1151.

21. Gofton WT, Gordon KD, Dunning CD, Johnson JA, King GJ. Soft-tissue stabilizers of the distal radioulnar joint: an in vitro kinematic study. J Hand Surg. 2004; 25(3):423-431.

22. Goubau JF, et al. The wrist hyperflexion and abduction of the thumb (WHAT) test: a more specific and sensitive test to diagnose de quervain tenosynovitis than the eichhoff's test. J Hand Surg (Eur). 2014; Mar;39(3):286-92.

23. Gupta V, Rijal L, Jawed A. Managing scaphoid fractures: how we do it? J Clin Orth and Trauma. 2013;4:3-10.

24. Hagert C-G. Stabilization of the distal radioulnar joint. In: Vastamäki M,ed. Current Trends in Hand Surgery. Amsterdam: Elsevier;1995:197-200.

25. Haase SC, Berger RA, Shin AY. Association between lunate morphology and carpal collapse patterns in scaphoid nonunions. J Hand Surg 2007; 32A:1009-1012.

26. Haugstvedt J, et al. Relative contributions of the ulnar attachments of the triangular fibrocartilage complex to the dynamic stability of the distal radioulnar joint. J Hand Surg. 2006; 31: 445-451.

27. Henry M. Arthroscopic management of dorsal wrist impingement. J Hand Surg 2008;33A:1201-1204.

28. Hultèn O. Ueber anatomische variationen der Handgelenkknochen. Ein Beitrag zur Kenntnis der Genese zwei verschiedener Mondbeinveränderungen. Acta Radiol. 1928;9:155.

29. Hollister AM, Dennerlein JT, Rempel DM. Passive resistance and mechanical advantage of the extensor mechanism. 6th Congress of the International Federation of Societies for Surgery of the Hand (Ifssh), 1995; 769-773.

30. Ishikawa J, Iwasaki N, Minami A. Influence of distal radioulnar joint subluxation on restricted forearm rotation after distal radius fracture. J Hand Surg. 2005; 30A:1178-1184.

31. Jung JM. Changes in ulnar variance in relation to forearm rotation and grip. J Bone Joint Surg. 2001; 83-B:1029-33.

32. Kaneko S, Takasaki H. Forearm pain diagnosed as intersection syndrome, managed by taping: a case series. J Orthop Sports Phys Ther 2011;41(7):514-519.

33. Kauer JMG. Anatomy and function of the wrist and hand. In: Gilula LA Yin Y eds. Imaging of the wrist and hand. Philadelphia, WB Saunders, 1996:48.

34. Kaufmann R et al. Kinematic of the midcarpal and radiocarpal joints in radioulnar deviation: an in vitro study. J Hand Surg 2005;30A: 937-942.

35. Kihara H, Palmer AK, Werner FW, Short WH, Fortino MD. The effect of dorsally angulated distal radius fractures on distal radioulnar joint congruency and forearm rotation. J Hand Surg.1996;21(A):40-47.

36. King GJW. Physical examination of the wrist. In: Gilula LA, Yin, Y (Eds) *Imaging of the wrist and hand,* Philadelphia, WB Sanders, 1996: 5-18.

37. Kleinman W. Stability of the distal radioulna joint: biomechanics, pathophysiology, physical diagnosis, and restoration of function. What we have learned in 25 years. J Hand Surg 2007; 32A (7):1086-1105.

38. Kolski MC, O'Connor A. A World of hurt: a guide to classifying pain. 2015. Thomas Land Publishers Inc.

39. Lanzetta M, Foucher G. Association of wartenberg's syndrome and de quervain's disease: a series of 26 cases. Plastic & Reconstructive Surgery. 1995; 96(2):408-12.

40. Lindau T, Adlercreutz C, Aspenberg P. Peripheral tears of the triangular fibrocartilage complex cause distal radioulnar joint instability after distal radial fractures. J Hand Surg 2000; 25A:464-468.

41. Linscheid RL. Biomechanics of the distal radioulnar joint. Clin Orthop.1992;275:46-54.

42. Lyritis G, Dimitracopoulos B, Nikolaou P, Gorgolis J. Functional disturbance of the inferior radio-ulnar joint due to hypoplasia of the lower end of the ulna. Prog Clin Biol Res. 1982;104:339-44.

43. Ma H & Kim I. The diagnostic assessment of hand elevation test in carpal tunnel syndrome. J Korean Neurosurg Soc. 2012;Nov; 52(5):472-475.

44. Marinus J, Moseley GL, Birklein F, Baron R, Maihöfner C, Kingery WS, & van Hilten JJ. Clinical features and pathophysiology of complex regional pain syndrome. Lancet neurol 2011:10 :637-48.

45. Marx RG, Bombardier C, Wright JG. What do we know about the reliability and validity of physical examination tests used to examine the upper extremity? J Hand Surg. 1999; 24A: 185-193.

46. McLean et al. Imaging of morphological variants at the midcarpal joint. J Hand Surg. 2009;34A:1044-1055.

47. McLean J et al. An anatomic study of the triquetrum-hamate joint. J Hand Surg 2006;31A:601–607.

48. Morimoto H, Viegas S, Elder KW, Nakamura K, DaSilva MF, Boyd NL, Patterson R. Scaphoid nonunions: A 3-dimensional analysis of patterns of deformity. J Hand Surg 2000; 25A: 520-528.

49. Moritomo H et al. IFSSH 2013 committee's report of wrist dart-throwing motion. J Hand Surg. Am. 2014; 39(7): 1433-1439.

50. Morimoto H et al. Change in the length of the ulnocarpal ligaments during radiocarpal motion: possible impact on triangular fibrocartilage complex   foveal tears. J Hand Surg. 2008; 33A:1278-1286.

51. Moriya T, Aoki M, Iba K, et al. Effect of triangular ligament tears on distal radioulnar joint instability and evaluation of three clinical tests: a biomechanical study. J Hand Surg. (European Vol) 2009; 34E:2:219-223.

52. Moseley, G. Graded motor imagery is effective for long-standing complex regional pain syndrome: a randomised controlled trial. Pain. 2004; 108: 192–198.

53. Moseley, G. Is successful rehabilitation of complex regional pain syndrome due to sustained attention to the affected limb? A randomised clinical trial. Pain. 2005; 114: 54–61.

54. Moseley, G. Graded Motor Imagery for pathologic pain. A randomized controlled trial. Neurology. 2006; 67:2129-34.

55. Moskal MJ, Savoie FH, Field LD. Arthroscopic capsulodesis of the lunatotriquetral joint. Clin Sports Med. 2001; 20:141-153.

56. Nagle DJ. Triangular fibrocartilage complex tears in the athlete. Clin Sports Med. 2001;20:155-65.

57. Nakamura K, Beppu M, , Patterson RM, Hanson CA, Hume PJ, Viegas SF. Motion analysis in two dimensions of radial-ulnar deviation of Type I versus Type II lunates. J Hand Surg 2000; 25A: 877-888.

58. Nakamura R, Horii T, Imaeda E, et al. The ulno-carpal stress test in the diagnosis of ulnar-sided wrist pain. J Hand Surg Br. 1997; 22: 719-723.

59. Nakamura T, Yabe Y, Horiuchi Y. Functional anatomy of the interosseous membrane of the forearm – dynamic changes during rotation. J Hand Surg 1999; 24B: 338-341.

60. Nakamura T et al. Radial styloidectomy: A biomechanical study on stability of the wrist joint. J Hand Surg 2001; 26-A: 85-93.

61. Netter FH. Atlas of human anatomy. CIBA-Geigy Corporation. Summit, NJ. 1996.

62. Nicolaidis SC et al. Acute injuries of the distal radioulnar joint. Hand Clinics 2000; 16:449-59.

63. Nishiwaki M, Nakamura T, Nakao Y, Nagura T, Toyama Y. Ulnar shortening effect on distal radioulnar joint stability: a biomechanical study. J Hand Surg 2005; 30A:719-726.

64. Neumann D. Kinesiology of the musculoskeletal system: foundations for physical rehabilitation. St. Louis: Mosby 2002.

65. Neumann D. Kinesiology of the musculoskeletal system: foundations for rehabilitation. 2nd Ed. St. Louis: Mosby 2010.

66. Noda K, Gotoa A, Murase T, Sugamoto K, Yoshikawa H, Moriomoto H. Interosseous membrane of the forearm: an anatomical study of the ligament attachment locations. J Hand Surg 2009; 34A:415-422.

67. Ombregt L. A system of orthopaedic medicine, 3rd ed. 2013. Churchill Livingstone Elsevier Ltd.

68. Palmer AK, Werner FW. Biomechanics of the distal radioulnar joint. Clin Orthop 1984;187:26-35.

69. Parvizi J, Wayman J, Kelly P, Morgan CG. Combining the clinical signs improves diagnosis of scaphoid fractures. A prospective study with follow up. J Hand Surg Br. 1998 Jun;23(3)324-7.

70. Porretto-Loehrke A. Taping techniques for the wrist. J Hand Ther. 2016; 29:213-216.

71. Primal Pictures ltd, 2006

72. Rayan GM. Pisiform ligament complex syndrome and pisotriquetral arthrosis. Hand Clin. 2005; 21:507–517.

73. Ring D, Jupiter JB. Acute Fractures of the Scaphoid. J Am Acad Orthop Surg 2000: 8: 225-31.

74. Rocchi L, Canal A, Fanfani F, Catalano F. Articular ganglia of the volar aspect of the wrist: Arthroscopic resection compared with open excision. A prospective randomized study. Scand J Plast Reconstr Surg Hand Surg, 2008;42:253-259.

75. Ruch DS. Arthroscopic assessment of carpal instability. Arthroscopy. 1998; 14:675-681.

76. Ruland RT & Hogan CJ. The ECU synergy test: an aide to diagnose ECU tendonitis. J Hand Surg. 2008; 33A: 1777-1782.

77. Sachar K. Ulnar-sided wrist pain: evaluation and treatment of triangular fibrocartilage complex tears, ulnocarpal impaction syndrome, and lunotriquetral ligament tears. J Hand Surg. 2008; 33A: 1669-1679.

78. Sauvé PS, Rhee PC, Shin AY, et al. Examination of the wrist: radial-sided wrist pain. J Hand Surg. 2014; Oct;39(10):2089-92.

79. Schuind FA, Linscheid RL, An K-N, Chao EYS. A normal database of posteroanterior measurements of the wrist. J Bone Joint Surg. 1992; 74A: 1418-1429.

80. Schuind FA, et al. The distal radio ulnar ligaments: A biomechanical study. J Hand Surg 1991; 16A:1106-1114.

81. Shen J, Papadonikolakis A, Garrett JP, Davis SM, Ruch DS. Ulnar-positive variance as a predictor of distal radioulnar joint ligament disruption. J Hand Surg 2005; 30A: 1172-1177.

82. Scheer JH and Adolfsson LE. Pathomechanisms of ulnar ligament lesions of the wrist in a cadaveric distal radius fracture model. Acta Orthopaedica. 2011; 82(3): 360-364.

83. Shin AY, Weinstein LP, Berger RA, Bishop AT. Treatment of isolated injuries in the lunatotriquetral ligament . J Bone Joint Surg. 2001;83-B:1023-28.

84. Stuart PR, Berger RA, Linscheid RL, An K. The dorsopalmar stability of the distal radioulnar joint. J Hand Surg 2000; 25A:689-699.

85. Taleisnik J, Watson HK. Midcarpal instability caused by malunited fractures of the distal radius. J Hand Surg. 1984; 9A:350-357.

86. Taleisnik, J., Linsheid, R. (1998) Scapholunate Instability. *The Wrist, Diagnosis and Optimal Treatment* (p.501-526). St. Louis: Mosby.

87. Tay SC, Tomita K, Berger R. The "ulnar fovea sign" for defining ulnar wrist pain: an analysis of sensitivity and specificity. J Hand Surg. 2007; 32A: 438-444.

88. Teefey SA, Dahiya N, Middleton WD, Gelberman RH, Boyer MI. Ganglia of the hand and wrist: A sonographic analysis. AJR 2008;191:716-720.

89. Trail IA, Linscheid RL. Pisiformectomy in young patients. J Hand Surg (Br). 1992; 17(3):346–348.

90. Trehan SK, Orbay JL, Wolfe SW. Coronal shift of distal radius fractures: influence of the distal interosseous membrane on distal radioulnar joint instability. J Hand Surg Am. 2015; 40:159-162.

91. Tsukazaki T. Ulnar wrist pain after Colles' Fracture. 109 fractures followed for 4 years. Acta Orth. Scand. 1993.

92. Valdes K & LaStayo P. The value of provocative tests for the wrist and elbow: a literature review. J Hand Ther. 2013; 26:32-42.

93. Vaught MS, et al. Association of disturbances in the thoracic outlet of subjects with carpal tunnel syndrome: A case-control study. J Hand Ther. 2011;24:44-52.

94. Viegas S., et al. (1999) The Dorsal Wrist Ligaments of the Wrist: Anatomy, Mechanical Properties, and Function. *J Hand Surg.*24A: 456-468.

95. Viegas S. Arthroscopic resection of dorsal wrist ganglia. Atlas Hand Clin. 2004: 199-206.

96. Viegas S, Yamaguchi S, Boyd, Patterson R. The dorsal ligaments of the wrist: Anatomy, mechanical properties, and function. J Hand Surg 1999; 24A: 456-468.

97. Wallwork NA, Bain GI. Sigmoid notch osteoplasty for chronic volar instability of the distal radioulnar joint: A case report. J Hand Surg 2001; 26A:454-459.

98. Wantanabe H, Berger R, An KN, Berglund LJ, Zobitz ME. Stability of the distal radioulnar joint contributed by the joint capsule. J Hand Surg 2004; 29A:1114-1120.

99. Wantanabe H, Berger R, Berglund LJ, Zobitz ME, An KN. Contribution of the interosseous membrane to distal radioulnar joint constraint. J Hand Surg 2005; 30A:1164-1171.

100. Wheeless' Textbook of Orthopaedics. WheelessOnline.com. Duke University Medical Center's Division of Orthopaedic Surgery, in conjunction with Data Trace Internet Publishing, LLC .

101. Wolfe SW, Neu C, Crisco JJ. In-vivo scaphoid, lunate, and capitate kinematics in flexion and extension. J Hand Surg 2000; 25-A:860-9.

102.   Wright, T., Michlovitz, S. (1996) Management of Carpal Instability. *J Hand Therapy.* 149-157.

103.   Wright TW, Glowczewskie F Jr, Cowin D, Wheeler DL. Radial nerve excursion and strain at the elbow and wrist associated with upper-extremity motion. J Hand Surg [Am]. 2005; 30(5):990-6.

104.   Xu J, Tang JB. In vivo changes in the lengths of the ligaments stabilizing   the distal radioulnar joint. J Hand Surgery 2009; 34A: 40-45.

105.   Yazaky N et al. Variations of capitate morphology in the wrist. J Hand Surg 2008;33A:660 – 666.

106.   Zancolli EA. Atlas of surgical anatomy of the hand. New York: Churchill-Livingstone; 1992:414.

Made in the USA
Middletown, DE
22 June 2018